MICHIGAN RULES (
PROCEDL
MICHIGAN RULES OF EVIDENCE

Revised on June 6, 2020
By West Hartford Legal Publishing

MICHIGAN SUPREME COURT

Table of Contents

Chapter 6. Criminal Procedure

Subchapter 6.000 General Provisions

Rule 6.001 Scope; Applicability of Civil Rules; Superseded Rules and Statutes

(A) Felony Cases. The rules in subchapters 6.000-6.500 govern matters of procedure in criminal cases cognizable in the circuit courts and in courts of equivalent criminal jurisdiction.

(B) Misdemeanor Cases. MCR 6.001-6.004, 6.005(B) and (C), 6.006, 6.101, 6.102(D) and (F), 6.103, 6.104(A), 6.106, 6.125, 6.202, 6.425(E)(3), 6.427, 6.430, 6.435, 6.440, 6.445(A)-(G), and the rules in subchapter 6.600 govern matters of procedure in criminal cases cognizable in the district courts.

(C) Juvenile Cases. The rules in subchapter 6.900 govern matters of procedure in the district courts and in circuit courts and courts of equivalent criminal jurisdiction in cases involving juveniles against whom the prosecutor has authorized the filing of a criminal complaint as provided in MCL 764.1f.

(D) Civil Rules Applicable. The provisions of the rules of civil procedure apply to cases governed by this chapter, except

(1) as otherwise provided by rule or statute,

(2) when it clearly appears that they apply to civil actions only,

(3) when a statute or court rule provides a like or different procedure, or

(4) with regard to limited appearances and notices of limited appearance.

Depositions and other discovery proceedings under subchapter 2.300 may not be taken for the purposes of discovery in cases governed by this chapter. The provisions of MCR 2.501(C) regarding the length of notice of trial assignment do not apply in cases governed by this chapter.

(E) Rules and Statutes Superseded. The rules in this chapter supersede all prior court rules in this chapter and any statutory procedure pertaining to and inconsistent with a procedure provided by a rule in this chapter.

Rule 6.002 Purpose and Construction

These rules are intended to promote a just determination of every criminal proceeding. They are to be construed to secure simplicity in procedure, fairness in administration, and the elimination of unjustifiable expense and delay.

Rule 6.003 Definitions

For purposes of subchapters 6.000-6.800:

(1) "Party" includes the lawyer representing the party.

(2) "Defendant's lawyer" includes a self-represented defendant proceeding without a lawyer.

(3) "Prosecutor" includes any lawyer prosecuting the case.

(4) "Court" or "judicial officer" includes a judge, a magistrate, or a district court magistrate authorized in accordance with the law to perform the functions of a magistrate.

(5) "Court clerk" includes a deputy clerk.

(6) "Court reporter" includes a court recorder.

RULE 6.004 SPEEDY TRIAL

(A) Right to Speedy Trial. The defendant and the people are entitled to a speedy trial and to a speedy resolution of all matters before the court. Whenever the defendant's constitutional right to a speedy trial is violated, the defendant is entitled to dismissal of the charge with prejudice.

(B) Priorities in Scheduling Criminal Cases. The trial court has the responsibility to establish and control a trial calendar. In assigning cases to the calendar, and insofar as it is practicable,

(1) the trial of criminal cases must be given preference over the trial of civil cases, and

(2) the trial of defendants in custody and of defendants whose pretrial liberty presents unusual risks must be given preference over other criminal cases.

(C) Delay in Felony and Misdemeanor Cases; Recognizance Release. In a felony case in which the defendant has been incarcerated for a period of 180 days or more to answer for the same crime or a crime based on the same conduct or arising from the same criminal episode, or in a misdemeanor case in which the defendant has been incarcerated for a period of 28 days or more to answer for the same crime or a crime based on the same conduct or arising from the same criminal episode, the defendant must be released on personal recognizance, unless the court finds by clear and convincing evidence that the defendant is likely either to fail to appear for future proceedings or to present a danger to any other person or the community. In computing the 28-day and 180-day periods, the court is to exclude

(1) periods of delay resulting from other proceedings concerning the defendant, including but not limited to competency and criminal responsibility proceedings, pretrial motions, interlocutory appeals, and the trial of other charges,

(2) the period of delay during which the defendant is not competent to stand trial,

(3) the period of delay resulting from an adjournment requested or consented to by the defendant's lawyer,

(4) the period of delay resulting from an adjournment requested by the prosecutor, but only if the prosecutor demonstrates on the record either

(a) the unavailability, despite the exercise of due diligence, of material evidence that the prosecutor has reasonable cause to believe will be available at a later date; or

(b) exceptional circumstances justifying the need for more time to prepare the state's case,

(5) a reasonable period of delay when the defendant is joined for trial with a codefendant as to whom the time for trial has not run, but only if good cause exists for not granting the defendant a severance so as to enable trial within the time limits applicable, and

(6) any other periods of delay that in the court's judgment are justified by good cause, but not including delay caused by docket congestion.

(D) Untried Charges Against State Prisoner.

(1) The 180-Day Rule. Except for crimes exempted by MCL 780.131(2), the inmate shall be brought to trial within 180 days after the department of corrections causes to be delivered to the prosecuting attorney of the county in which the warrant,

indictment, information, or complaint is pending written notice of the place of imprisonment of the inmate and a request for final disposition of the warrant, indictment, information, or complaint. The request shall be accompanied by a statement setting forth the term of commitment under which the prisoner is being held, the time already served, the time remaining to be served on the sentence, the amount of good time or disciplinary credits earned, the time of parole eligibility of the prisoner, and any decisions of the parole board relating to the prisoner. The written notice and statement shall be delivered by certified mail.

(2) Remedy. In the event that action is not commenced on the matter for which request for disposition was made as required in subsection (1), no court of this state shall any longer have jurisdiction thereof, nor shall the untried warrant, indictment, information, or complaint be of any further force or effect, and the court shall enter an order dismissing the same with prejudice.

RULE 6.005 RIGHT TO ASSISTANCE OF LAWYER; ADVICE; APPOINTMENT FOR INDIGENTS; WAIVER; JOINT REPRESENTATION; GRAND JURY PROCEEDINGS

(A) Advice of Right. At the arraignment on the warrant or complaint, the court must advise the defendant

(1) of entitlement to a lawyer's assistance at all subsequent court proceedings, and

(2) that the court will appoint a lawyer at public expense if the defendant wants one and is financially unable to retain one.

The court must question the defendant to determine whether the defendant wants a lawyer and, if so, whether the defendant is financially unable to retain one.

(B) Questioning Defendant About Indigency. If the defendant requests a lawyer and claims financial inability to retain one, the court must determine whether the defendant is indigent. The determination of indigency must be guided by the following factors:

(1) present employment, earning capacity and living expenses;

(2) outstanding debts and liabilities, secured and unsecured;

(3) whether the defendant has qualified for and is receiving any form of public assistance;

(4) availability and convertibility, without undue financial hardship to the defendant and the defendant's dependents, of any personal or real property owned; and

(5) any other circumstances that would impair the ability to pay a lawyer's fee as would ordinarily be required to retain competent counsel.

The ability to post bond for pretrial release does not make the defendant ineligible for appointment of a lawyer.

(C) Partial Indigency. If a defendant is able to pay part of the cost of a lawyer, the court may require contribution to the cost of providing a lawyer and may establish a plan for collecting the contribution.

(D) Appointment or Waiver of a Lawyer. If the court determines that the defendant is financially unable to retain a lawyer, it must promptly appoint a lawyer and promptly notify the lawyer of the appointment. The court may not permit the defendant to make an initial waiver of the right to be represented by a lawyer without first

(1) advising the defendant of the charge, the maximum possible prison sentence for the offense, any mandatory minimum sentence required by law, and the risk involved in self-representation, and

11

(2) offering the defendant the opportunity to consult with a retained lawyer or, if the defendant is indigent, the opportunity to consult with an appointed lawyer.

(E) Advice at Subsequent Proceedings. If a defendant has waived the assistance of a lawyer, the record of each subsequent proceeding (e.g., preliminary examination, arraignment, proceedings leading to possible revocation of youthful trainee status, hearings, trial or sentencing) need show only that the court advised the defendant of the continuing right to a lawyer's assistance (at public expense if the defendant is indigent) and that the defendant waived that right. Before the court begins such proceedings,

(1) the defendant must reaffirm that a lawyer's assistance is not wanted; or

(2) if the defendant requests a lawyer and is financially unable to retain one, the court must appoint one; or

(3) if the defendant wants to retain a lawyer and has the financial ability to do so, the court must allow the defendant a reasonable opportunity to retain one.

The court may refuse to adjourn a proceeding to appoint counsel or allow a defendant to retain counsel if an adjournment would significantly prejudice the prosecution, and the defendant has not been reasonably diligent in seeking counsel.

(F) Multiple Representation. When two or more indigent defendants are jointly charged with an offense or offenses or their cases are otherwise joined, the court must appoint separate lawyers unassociated in the practice of law for each defendant. Whenever two or more defendants who have been jointly charged or whose cases have been joined are represented by the same retained lawyer or lawyers associated in the practice of law, the court must inquire into the potential for a conflict of interest that might jeopardize the right of each defendant to the undivided loyalty of the lawyer. The court may not permit the joint representation unless:

(1) the lawyer or lawyers state on the record the reasons for believing that joint representation in all probability will not cause a conflict of interests;

(2) the defendants state on the record after the court's inquiry and the lawyer's statement, that they desire to proceed with the same lawyer; and

(3) the court finds on the record that joint representation in all probability will not cause a conflict of interest and states its reasons for the finding.

(G) Unanticipated Conflict of Interest. If, in a case of joint representation, a conflict of interest arises at any time, including trial, the lawyer must immediately inform the court. If the court agrees that a conflict has arisen, it must afford one or more of the defendants the opportunity to retain separate lawyers. The court should on its own initiative inquire into any potential conflict that becomes apparent, and take such action as the interests of justice require.

(H) Scope of Trial Lawyer's Responsibilities. The responsibilities of the trial lawyer who represents the defendant include

(1) representing the defendant in all trial court proceedings through initial sentencing,

(2) filing of interlocutory appeals the lawyer deems appropriate, and

(3) responding to any preconviction appeals by the prosecutor. The defendant's lawyer must either:

(i) file a substantive brief in response to the prosecutor's interlocutory application for leave to appeal, or

(ii) notify the Court of Appeals that the lawyer will not be filing a brief in response to the application.

(4) Unless an appellate lawyer has been appointed or retained, or if retained trial counsel withdraws, the trial lawyer who represents the defendant is responsible for filing postconviction motions the lawyer deems appropriate, including motions for new trial, for a directed verdict of acquittal, to withdraw plea, or for resentencing.

(5) when an appellate lawyer has been appointed or retained, promptly making the defendant's file, including all discovery material obtained, available for copying upon request of that lawyer. The trial lawyer must retain the materials in the defendant's file for at least five years after the case is disposed in the trial court.

(I) Assistance of Lawyer at Grand Jury Proceedings.

(1) A witness called before a grand jury or a grand juror is entitled to have a lawyer present in the hearing room while the witness gives testimony. A witness may not refuse to appear for reasons of unavailability of the lawyer for that witness. Except as otherwise provided by law, the lawyer may not participate in the proceedings other than to advise the witness.

(2) The prosecutor assisting the grand jury is responsible for ensuring that a witness is informed of the right to a lawyer's assistance during examination by written notice accompanying the subpoena to the witness and by personal advice immediately before the examination. The notice must include language informing the witness that if the witness is financially unable to retain a lawyer, the chief judge in the circuit court in which the grand jury is convened will on request appoint one for the witness at public expense.

RULE 6.006 VIDEO AND AUDIO PROCEEDINGS

(A) Defendant in the Courtroom or at a Separate Location. District and circuit courts may use two-way interactive video technology to conduct the following proceedings between a courtroom and a prison, jail, or other location: initial arraignments on the warrant or complaint, probable cause conferences, arraignments on the information, pretrial conferences, pleas, sentencings for misdemeanor offenses, show cause hearings, waivers and adjournments of extradition, referrals for forensic determination of competency, waivers and adjournments of preliminary examinations, and hearings on postjudgment motions to amend restitution.

(B) Defendant in the Courtroom - Preliminary Examinations. As long as the defendant is either present in the courtroom or has waived the right to be present, on motion of either party, district courts may use telephonic, voice, or video conferencing, including two-way interactive video technology, to take testimony from an expert witness or, upon a showing of good cause, any person at another location in a preliminary examination.

(C) Defendant in the Courtroom - Other Proceedings. As long as the defendant is either present in the courtroom or has waived the right to be present, upon a showing of good cause, district and circuit courts may use videoconferencing technology to take testimony from a person at another location in the following proceedings:

(1) evidentiary hearings, competency hearings, sentencings, probation revocation proceedings, and proceedings to revoke a sentence that does not entail an adjudication of guilt, such as youthful trainee status;

(2) with the consent of the parties, trials. A party who does not consent to the use of videoconferencing technology to take testimony from a person at trial shall not be required to articulate any reason for not consenting.

(D) Mechanics of Use. The use of telephonic, voice, video conferencing, or two-way interactive video technology, must be in accordance with any requirements and guidelines established by the State Court Administrative Office, and all proceedings at which such technology is used must be recorded verbatim by the court.

RULE 6.007 CONFIDENTIAL RECORDS

Records are public except as otherwise indicated in court rule or statute.

RULE 6.008 CRIMINAL JURISDICTION

(A) District Court. The district court has jurisdiction over all misdemeanors and all felonies through the preliminary examination and until the entry of an order to bind the defendant over to the circuit court.

(B) Circuit Court. The circuit court has jurisdiction over all felonies from the bindover from the district court unless otherwise provided by law. The failure of the court to properly document the bindover decision shall not deprive the circuit court of jurisdiction. A party challenging a bindover decision must do so before any plea of guilty or no contest, or before trial.

(C) Pleas and Verdicts in Circuit Court. The circuit court retains jurisdiction over any case in which a plea is entered or a verdict rendered to a charge that would normally be cognizable in the district court.

(D) Sentencing Misdemeanors in Circuit Court. The circuit court shall sentence all defendants bound over to circuit court on a felony that either plead guilty to, or are found guilty of, a misdemeanor.

(E) Concurrent Jurisdiction. As part of a concurrent jurisdiction plan, the circuit court and district court may enter into an agreement for district court probation officers to prepare the presentence investigation report and supervise on probation defendants who either plead guilty to, or are found guilty of, a misdemeanor in circuit court. The case remains under the jurisdiction of the circuit court.

Subchapter 6.100 Preliminary Proceedings

Rule 6.101 Complaint

(A) Definition and Form. A complaint is a written accusation that a named or described person has committed a specified criminal offense. The complaint must include the substance of the accusation against the accused and the name and statutory citation of the offense. At the time of filing, specified case initiation information shall be provided in the form and manner approved by the State Court Administrative Office.

(B) Signature and Oath. The complaint must be signed and verified under MCR 1.109(D)(3). Any requirement of law that a complaint filed with the court must be sworn is met by this verification.

(C) Prosecutor's Approval or Posting of Security. A complaint may not be filed without a prosecutor's written approval endorsed on the complaint or attached to it, or unless security for costs is filed with the court.

RULE 6.102 ARREST ON A WARRANT

(A) Issuance of Warrant. A court must issue an arrest warrant, or a summons in accordance with MCR 6.103, if presented with a proper complaint and if the court finds probable cause to believe that the accused committed the alleged offense.

(B) Probable Cause Determination. A finding of probable cause may be based on hearsay evidence and rely on factual allegations in the complaint, affidavits from the complainant or others, the testimony of a sworn witness adequately preserved to permit review, or any combination of these sources.

(C) Contents of Warrant; Court's Subscription. A warrant must

(1) contain the accused's name, if known, or an identifying name or description;

(2) describe the offense charged in the complaint;

(3) command a peace officer or other person authorized by law to arrest and bring the accused before a judicial officer of the judicial district in which the offense allegedly was committed or some other designated court; and

(4) be signed by the court.

(D) Warrant Specification of Interim Bail. Where permitted by law, the court may specify on the warrant the bail that an accused may post to obtain release before arraignment on the warrant and, if the court deems it appropriate, include as a bail condition that the arrest of the accused occur on or before a specified date or within a specified period of time after issuance of the warrant.

(E) Execution and Return of Warrant. Only a peace officer or other person authorized by law may execute an arrest warrant. On execution or attempted execution of the warrant, the officer must make a return on the warrant and deliver it to the court before which the arrested person is to be taken.

(F) Release on Interim Bail. If an accused has been arrested pursuant to a warrant that includes an interim bail provision, the accused must either be arraigned promptly or released pursuant to the interim bail provision. The accused may obtain release by posting the bail on the warrant and by submitting a recognizance to appear before a specified court at a specified date and time, provided that

(1) the accused is arrested prior to the expiration date, if any, of the bail provision;

(2) the accused is arrested in the county in which the warrant was issued, or in which the accused resides or is employed, and the accused is not wanted on another charge;

(3) the accused is not under the influence of liquor or controlled substance; and

(4) the condition of the accused or the circumstances at the time of arrest do not otherwise suggest a need for judicial review of the original specification of bail.

RULE 6.103 SUMMONS INSTEAD OF ARREST

(A) Issuance of Summons. If the prosecutor so requests, the court may issue a summons instead of an arrest warrant. If an accused fails to appear in response to a summons, the court, on request, must issue an arrest warrant.

(B) Form. A summons must contain the same information as an arrest warrant, except that it should summon the accused to appear before a designated court at a stated time and place.

(C) Service and Return of Summons. A summons may be served by

(1) delivering a copy to the named individual; or

(2) leaving a copy with a person of suitable age and discretion at the individual's home or usual place of abode; or

(3) mailing a copy to the individual's last known address.

Service should be made promptly to give the accused adequate notice of the appearance date. The person serving the summons must make a return to the court before which the person is summoned to appear.

(A) Arraignment Without Unnecessary Delay. Unless released beforehand, an arrested person must be taken without unnecessary delay before a court for arraignment in accordance with the provisions of this rule, or must be arraigned without unnecessary delay by use of two-way interactive video technology in accordance with MCR 6.006(A).

(B) Place of Arraignment. An accused arrested pursuant to a warrant must be taken to a court specified in the warrant. An accused arrested without a warrant must be taken to a court in the judicial district in which the offense allegedly occurred. If the arrest occurs outside the county in which these courts are located, the arresting agency must make arrangements with the authorities in the demanding county to have the accused promptly transported to the latter county for arraignment in accordance with the provisions of this rule. If prompt transportation cannot be arranged, the accused must be taken without unnecessary delay before the nearest available court for preliminary appearance in accordance with subrule (C). In the alternative, the provisions of this subrule may be satisfied by use of two-way interactive video technology in accordance with MCR 6.006(A).

(C) Preliminary Appearance Outside County of Offense. When, under subrule (B), an accused is taken before a court outside the county of the alleged offense either in person or by way of two-way interactive video technology, the court must advise the accused of the rights specified in subrule (E)(2) and determine what form of pretrial release, if any, is appropriate. To be released, the accused must submit a recognizance for appearance within the next 14 days before a court specified in the arrest warrant or, in a case involving an arrest without a warrant, before either a court in the judicial district in which the offense allegedly occurred or some other court designated by that court. The court must certify the recognizance and have it delivered or sent without delay to the appropriate court. If the accused is not released, the arresting agency must arrange prompt transportation to the judicial district of the offense. In all cases, the arraignment is then to continue under subrule (D), if applicable, and subrule (E) either in the judicial district of the alleged offense or in such court as otherwise is designated.

(D) Arrest Without Warrant. If an accused is arrested without a warrant, a complaint complying with MCR 6.101 must be filed at or before the time of arraignment. On receiving the complaint and on finding probable cause, the court must either issue a warrant or endorse the complaint as provided in MCL 764.1c. Arraignment of the accused may then proceed in accordance with subrule (E).

(E) Arraignment Procedure; Judicial Responsibilities. The court at the arraignment must
    (1) inform the accused of the nature of the offense charged, and its maximum possible prison sentence and any mandatory minimum sentence required by law;
    (2) if the accused is not represented by a lawyer at the arraignment, advise the accused that
        (a) the accused has a right to remain silent,
        (b) anything the accused says orally or in writing can be used against the accused in court,
        (c) the accused has a right to have a lawyer present during any questioning consented to, and
        (d) if the accused does not have the money to hire a lawyer, the court will appoint a lawyer for the accused;

(3) advise the accused of the right to a lawyer at all subsequent court proceedings and, if appropriate, appoint a lawyer;

(4) set a date for a probable cause conference not less than 7 days or more than 14 days after the date of the arraignment and set a date for preliminary examination not less than 5 days or more than 7 days after the date of the probable cause conference;

(5) determine what form of pretrial release, if any, is appropriate; and

(6) ensure that the accused has had biometric data collected as required by law.

The court may not question the accused about the alleged offense or request that the accused enter a plea.

(F) Arraignment Procedure; Recording. A verbatim record must be made of the arraignment.

(G) Plan for Judicial Availability. In each county, the court with trial jurisdiction over felony cases must adopt and file with the state court administrator a plan for judicial availability. The plan shall

(1) make a judicial officer available for arraignments each day of the year, or

(2) make a judicial officer available for setting bail for every person arrested for commission of a felony each day of the year conditioned upon

(a) the judicial officer being presented a proper complaint and finding probable cause pursuant to MCR 6.102(A), and

(b) the judicial officer having available information to set bail.

This portion of the plan must provide that the judicial officer shall order the arresting officials to arrange prompt transportation of any accused unable to post bond to the judicial district of the offense for arraignment not later than the next regular business day.

RULE 6.106 PRETRIAL RELEASE

(A) In General. At the defendant's arraignment on the complaint and/or warrant, unless an order in accordance with this rule was issued beforehand, the court must order that, pending trial, the defendant be

(1) held in custody as provided in subrule (B);

(2) released on personal recognizance or an unsecured appearance bond; or

(3) released conditionally, with or without money bail (ten percent, cash or surety).

(B) Pretrial Release/Custody Order Under Const 1963, art 1, § 15.

(1) The court may deny pretrial release to

(a) a defendant charged with

(i) murder or treason, or

(ii) committing a violent felony and

[A] at the time of the commission of the violent felony, the defendant was on probation, parole, or released pending trial for another violent felony, or

[B] during the 15 years preceding the commission of the violent felony, the defendant had been convicted of 2 or more violent felonies under the laws of this state or substantially similar laws of the United States or another state arising out of separate incidents, if the court finds that proof of the defendant's guilt is evident or the presumption great;

(b) a defendant charged with criminal sexual conduct in the first degree, armed robbery, or kidnapping with the intent to extort money or other valuable thing thereby, if the court finds that proof of the defendant's guilt is evident or the presumption great, unless the court finds by clear and convincing evidence that the defendant is not likely to flee or present a danger to any other person.

(2) A "violent felony" within the meaning of subrule (B)(1) is a felony, an element of which involves a violent act or threat of a violent act against any other person.

(3) If the court determines as provided in subrule (B)(1) that the defendant may not be released, the court must order the defendant held in custody for a period not to exceed 90 days after the date of the order, excluding delays attributable to the defense, within which trial must begin or the court must immediately schedule a hearing and set the amount of bail.

(4) The court must state the reasons for an order of custody on the record and on a form approved by the State Court Administrator's Office entitled "Custody Order." The completed form must be placed in the court file.

(5) The court may, in its custody order, place conditions on the defendant, including but not limited to restricting or prohibiting defendant's contact with any other named person or persons, if the court determines the conditions are reasonably necessary to maintain the integrity of the judicial proceedings or are reasonably necessary for the protection of one or more named persons. If an order under this paragraph is in conflict with another court order, the most restrictive provisions of the orders shall take precedence until the conflict is resolved.

(6) Nothing in this rule limits the ability of a jail to impose restrictions on detainee contact as an appropriate means of furthering penological goals.

(C) Release on Personal Recognizance. If the defendant is not ordered held in custody pursuant to subrule (B), the court must order the pretrial release of the defendant on personal recognizance, or on an unsecured appearance bond, subject to the conditions that the defendant will appear as required, will not leave the state without permission of the court, and will not commit any crime while released, unless the court determines that such release will not reasonably ensure the appearance of the defendant as required, or that such release will present a danger to the public.

(D) Conditional Release. If the court determines that the release described in subrule (C) will not reasonably ensure the appearance of the defendant as required, or will not reasonably ensure the safety of the public, the court may order the pretrial release of the defendant on the condition or combination of conditions that the court determines are appropriate including

(1) that the defendant will appear as required, will not leave the state without permission of the court, and will not commit any crime while released, and

(2) subject to any condition or conditions the court determines are reasonably necessary to ensure the appearance of the defendant as required and the safety of the public, which may include requiring the defendant to

(a) make reports to a court agency as are specified by the court or the agency;

(b) not use alcohol or illicitly use any controlled substance;

(c) participate in a substance abuse testing or monitoring program;

(d) participate in a specified treatment program for any physical or mental condition, including substance abuse;

(e) comply with restrictions on personal associations, place of residence, place of employment, or travel;

(f) surrender driver's license or passport;

(g) comply with a specified curfew;

(h) continue to seek employment;

(i) continue or begin an educational program;

(j) remain in the custody of a responsible member of the community who agrees to monitor the defendant and report any violation of any release condition to the court;

(k) not possess a firearm or other dangerous weapon;

(l) not enter specified premises or areas and not assault, beat, molest or wound a named person or persons;

(m) comply with any condition limiting or prohibiting contact with any other named person or persons. If an order under this paragraph limiting or prohibiting contact with any other named person or persons is in conflict with another court order, the most restrictive provision of the orders shall take precedence until the conflict is resolved. The court may make this condition effective immediately on entry of a pretrial release order and while defendant remains in custody if the court determines it is reasonably necessary to maintain the integrity of the judicial proceeding or it is reasonably necessary for the protection of one or more named persons.

(n) satisfy any injunctive order made a condition of release; or

(o) comply with any other condition, including the requirement of money bail as described in subrule (E), reasonably necessary to ensure the defendant's appearance as required and the safety of the public.

(E) Money Bail. If the court determines for reasons it states on the record that the defendant's appearance or the protection of the public cannot otherwise be assured, money bail, with or without conditions described in subrule (D), may be required.

(1) The court may require the defendant to

(a) post, at the defendant's option,

(i) a surety bond that is executed by a surety approved by the court in an amount equal to 1/4 of the full bail amount, or

(ii) bail that is executed by the defendant, or by another who is not a surety approved by the court, and secured by

[A] a cash deposit, or its equivalent, for the full bail amount, or

[B] a cash deposit of 10 percent of the full bail amount, or, with the court's consent,

[C] designated real property; or

(b) post, at the defendant's option,

(i) a surety bond that is executed by a surety approved by the court in an amount equal to the full bail amount, or

(ii) bail that is executed by the defendant, or by another who is not a surety approved by the court, and secured by

[A] a cash deposit, or its equivalent, for the full bail amount, or, with the court's consent,

[B] designated real property.

(2) The court may require satisfactory proof of value and interest in property if the court consents to the posting of a bond secured by designated real property.

(F) Decision; Statement of Reasons.

(1) In deciding which release to use and what terms and conditions to impose, the court is to consider relevant information, including

(a) defendant's prior criminal record, including juvenile offenses;

(b) defendant's record of appearance or nonappearance at court proceedings or flight to avoid prosecution;

(c) defendant's history of substance abuse or addiction;

(d) defendant's mental condition, including character and reputation for dangerousness;

(e) the seriousness of the offense charged, the presence or absence of threats, and the probability of conviction and likely sentence;

(f) defendant's employment status and history and financial history insofar as these factors relate to the ability to post money bail;

(g) the availability of responsible members of the community who would vouch for or monitor the defendant;

(h) facts indicating the defendant's ties to the community, including family ties and relationships, and length of residence, and

(i) any other facts bearing on the risk of nonappearance or danger to the public.

(2) If the court orders the defendant held in custody pursuant to subrule (B) or released on conditions in subrule (D) that include money bail, the court must state the reasons for its decision on the record. The court need not make a finding on each of the enumerated factors.

(3) Nothing in subrules (C) through (F) may be construed to sanction pretrial detention nor to sanction the determination of pretrial release on the basis of race, religion, gender, economic status, or other impermissible criteria.

(G) Custody Hearing.

(1) Entitlement to Hearing. A court having jurisdiction of a defendant may conduct a custody hearing if the defendant is being held in custody pursuant to subrule (B) and a custody hearing is requested by either the defendant or the prosecutor. The purpose of the hearing is to permit the parties to litigate all of the issues relevant to challenging or supporting a custody decision pursuant to subrule (B).

(2) Hearing Procedure.

(a) At the custody hearing, the defendant is entitled to be present and to be represented by a lawyer, and the defendant and the prosecutor are entitled to present witnesses and evidence, to proffer information, and to cross-examine each other's witnesses.

(b) The rules of evidence, except those pertaining to privilege, are not applicable. Unless the court makes the findings required to enter an order under subrule (B)(1), the defendant must be ordered released under subrule (C) or (D). A verbatim record of the hearing must be made.

(H) Appeals; Modification of Release Decision.

(1) Appeals. A party seeking review of a release decision may file a motion in the court having appellate jurisdiction over the court that made the release decision. There is no fee for filing the motion. The reviewing court may not stay, vacate, modify, or reverse the release decision except on finding an abuse of discretion.

(2) Modification of Release Decision.

(a) Prior to Arraignment on the Information. Prior to the defendant's arraignment on the information, any court before which proceedings against the defendant are pending may, on the motion of a party or its own initiative and on finding that there is a substantial reason for doing so, modify a prior release decision or reopen a prior custody hearing.

(b) Arraignment on Information and Afterwards. At the defendant's arraignment on the information and afterwards, the court having jurisdiction of the defendant may, on the motion of a party or its own initiative, make a de novo determination and modify a prior release decision or reopen a prior custody hearing.

(c) Burden of Going Forward. The party seeking modification of a release decision has the burden of going forward.

(3) Emergency Release. If a defendant being held in pretrial custody under this rule is ordered released from custody as a result of a court order or law requiring the release of prisoners to relieve jail conditions, the court ordering the defendant's release may, if appropriate, impose conditions of release in accordance with this rule to ensure the appearance of the defendant as required and to protect the public. If such conditions of release are imposed, the court must inform the defendant of the conditions on the record or by furnishing to the defendant or the defendant's lawyer a copy of the release order setting forth the conditions.

(I) Termination of Release Order.

(1) If the conditions of the release order are met and the defendant is discharged from all obligations in the case, the court must vacate the release order, discharge anyone who has posted bail or bond, and return the cash (or its equivalent) posted in the full amount of the bail, or, if there has been a deposit of 10 percent of the full bail amount, return 90 percent of the deposited money and retain 10 percent.

(2) If the defendant has failed to comply with the conditions of release, the court may issue a warrant for the arrest of the defendant and enter an order revoking the release order and declaring the bail money deposited or the surety bond, if any, forfeited.

(a) The court must mail notice of any revocation order immediately to the defendant at the defendant's last known address and, if forfeiture of bail or bond has been ordered, to anyone who posted bail or bond.

(b) If the defendant does not appear and surrender to the court within 28 days after the revocation date, the court may continue the revocation order and enter judgment for the state or local unit of government against the defendant and anyone who posted bail or bond for an amount not to exceed the full amount of the bail, and costs of the court proceedings, or if a surety bond was posted, an amount not to exceed the full amount of the surety bond. If the amount of a forfeited surety bond is less than the full amount of the bail, the defendant shall continue to be liable to the court for the difference, unless otherwise ordered by the court. If the defendant does not within that period satisfy the court that there was compliance with the conditions of release other than appearance or that compliance was impossible through no fault of the defendant, the court may continue the revocation order and enter judgment for the state or local unit of government against the defendant alone for an amount not to exceed the full amount of the bond, and costs of the court proceedings.

(c) The 10 percent bail deposit made under subrule (E)(1)(a)(ii)[B] must be applied to the costs and, if any remains, to the balance of the judgment. The amount applied to the judgment must be transferred to the county treasury for a circuit court case, to the treasuries of the governments contributing to the district control unit for a district court case, or to the treasury of the appropriate municipal government for a municipal court case. The balance of the judgment may be enforced and collected as a judgment entered in a civil case.

(3) If money was deposited on a bail or bond executed by the defendant, the money must be first applied to the amount of any fine, costs, or statutory assessments imposed and any balance returned, subject to subrule (I)(1).

RULE 6.107 GRAND JURY PROCEEDINGS

(A) Right to Grand Jury Records. Whenever an indictment is returned by a grand jury or a grand juror, the person accused in the indictment is entitled to the part of the record, including a transcript of the part of the testimony of all witnesses appearing before the grand jury or grand juror, that touches on the guilt or innocence of the accused of the charge contained in the indictment.

(B) Procedure to Obtain Records.

(1) To obtain the part of the record and transcripts specified in subrule (A), a motion must be addressed to the chief judge of the circuit court in the county in which the grand jury issuing the indictment was convened.

(2) The motion must be filed within 14 days after arraignment on the indictment or at a reasonable time thereafter as the court may permit on a showing of good cause and a finding that the interests of justice will be served.

(3) On receipt of the motion, the chief judge shall order the entire record and transcript of testimony taken before the grand jury to be delivered to the chief judge by the person having custody of it for an in-camera inspection by the chief judge.

(4) Following the in-camera inspection, the chief judge shall certify the parts of the record, including the testimony of all grand jury witnesses that touches on the guilt or innocence of the accused, as being all of the evidence bearing on that issue contained in the record, and have two copies of it prepared, one to be delivered to the attorney for the accused, or to the accused if not represented by an attorney, and one to the attorney charged with the responsibility for prosecuting the indictment.

(5) The chief judge shall then have the record and transcript of all testimony of grand jury witnesses returned to the person from whom it was received for disposition according to law.

RULE 6.108 THE PROBABLE CAUSE CONFERENCE

(A) Right to a probable Cause Conference. The state and the defendant are entitled to a probable cause conference, unless waived by both parties. If the probable cause conference is waived, the parties shall provide written notice to the court and indicate whether the parties will be conducting a preliminary examination, waiving the examination, or entering a plea.

(B) A district court magistrate may conduct probable cause conferences when authorized to do so by the chief district judge and may conduct all matters allowed at the probable cause conference, except taking pleas and imposing sentences unless permitted by statute to take pleas or impose sentences.

(C) The probable cause conference shall include discussions regarding a possible plea agreement and other pretrial matters, including bail and bond modification.

(D) The district court judge must be available during the probable cause conference to take pleas, consider requests for modification of bond, and if requested by the prosecutor, take the testimony of a victim.

(E) The probable cause conference for codefendants who are arraigned at least 72 hours before the probable cause conference shall be consolidated and only one joint probable cause conference shall be held unless the prosecuting attorney consents to the severance, a defendant seeks severance by motion and it is granted, or one of the defendants is unavailable and does not appear at the hearing.

RULE 6.110 THE PRELIMINARY EXAMINATION

(A) Right to Preliminary Examination. Where a preliminary examination is permitted by law, the people and the defendant are entitled to a prompt preliminary examination. The defendant may waive the preliminary examination with the consent of the prosecuting attorney. Upon waiver of the preliminary examination, the court must bind the defendant over for trial on the charge set forth in the complaint or any amended complaint. The preliminary examination for codefendants shall be consolidated and only one joint preliminary examination shall be held unless the prosecuting attorney consents to the severance, a defendant seeks severance by motion and it is granted, or one of the defendants is unavailable and does not appear at the hearing.

(B) Time of Examination; Remedy.

(1) Unless adjourned by the court, the preliminary examination must be held on the date specified by the court at the arraignment on the warrant or complaint. If the parties consent, the court may adjourn the preliminary examination for a reasonable time. If a party objects, the court may not adjourn a preliminary examination unless it makes a finding on the record of good cause shown for the adjournment. A violation of this subrule is deemed to be harmless error unless the defendant demonstrates actual prejudice.

(2) Upon the request of the prosecuting attorney, the preliminary examination shall commence immediately at the date and time set for the probable cause conference for the sole purpose of taking and preserving the testimony of the victim, if the victim is present, as long as the defendant is either present in the courtroom or has waived the right to be present. If victim testimony is taken as provided under this rule, the preliminary examination will be continued at the date originally set for that event.

(C) Conduct of Examination. A verbatim record must be made of the preliminary examination. Each party may subpoena witnesses, offer proofs, and examine and cross-examine witnesses at the preliminary examination. The court must conduct the examination in accordance with the Michigan Rules of Evidence.

(D) Exclusionary Rules.

(1) The court shall allow the prosecutor and defendant to subpoena and call witnesses from whom hearsay testimony was introduced on a satisfactory showing that live testimony will be relevant.

(2) If, during the preliminary examination, the court determines that evidence being offered is excludable, it must, on motion or objection, exclude the evidence. If, however, there has been a preliminary showing that the evidence is admissible, the court need not hold a separate evidentiary hearing on the question of whether the evidence should be excluded. The decision to admit or exclude evidence, with or without an evidentiary hearing, does not preclude a party from moving for and obtaining a determination of the question in the trial court on the basis of

(a) a prior evidentiary hearing, or

(b) a prior evidentiary hearing supplemented with a hearing before the trial court, or

(c) if there was no prior evidentiary hearing, a new evidentiary hearing.

(E) Probable Cause Finding. If, after considering the evidence, the court determines that probable cause exists to believe both that an offense not cognizable by the district court has been committed and that the defendant committed it, the court must bind the defendant over for trial. If the court finds probable cause to believe that the defendant has committed an offense cognizable by the district court, it must proceed thereafter as if the defendant initially had been charged with that offense.

(F) Discharge of Defendant. No Finding of Probable Cause. If, after considering the evidence, the court determines that probable cause does not exist to believe either that an offense has been committed or that the defendant committed it, the court must discharge the defendant without prejudice to the prosecutor initiating a subsequent prosecution for the same offense or reduce the charge to an offense that is not a felony. Except as provided in MCR 8.111(C), the subsequent preliminary examination must be held before the same judicial officer and the prosecutor must present additional evidence to support the charge.

(G) Return of Examination. Immediately on concluding the examination, the court must certify and transmit to the court before which the defendant is bound to appear the prosecutor's authorization for a warrant application, the complaint, a copy of the register of actions, the examination return, and any recognizances received.

(H) Motion to Dismiss. If, on proper motion, the trial court finds a violation of subrule (C), (D), (E), or (F), it must either dismiss the information or remand the case to the district court for further proceedings.

(I) Scheduling the Arraignment. Unless the trial court does the scheduling of the arraignment on the information, the district court must do so in accordance with the administrative orders of the trial court.

RULE 6.111 CIRCUIT COURT ARRAIGNMENT IN DISTRICT COURT

(A) The circuit court arraignment may be conducted by a district judge in criminal cases cognizable in the circuit court immediately after the bindover of the defendant. A district court judge shall take a felony plea as provided by court rule if a plea agreement is reached between the parties. Following a plea, the case shall be transferred to the circuit court where the circuit judge shall preside over further proceedings, including sentencing. The circuit court judge's name shall be available to the litigants before the plea is taken.

(B) Arraignments conducted pursuant to this rule shall be conducted in conformity with MCR 6.113.

(C) Pleas taken pursuant to this rule shall be taken in conformity with MCR 6.301, 6.302, 6.303, and 6.304, as applicable, and, once taken, shall be governed by MCR 6.310.

RULE 6.112 THE INFORMATION OR INDICTMENT

(A) Informations and Indictments; Similar Treatment. Except as otherwise provided in these rules or elsewhere, the law and rules that apply to informations and prosecutions on informations apply to indictments and prosecutions on indictments.

(B) Use of Information or Indictment. A prosecution must be based on an information or an indictment. Unless the defendant is a fugitive from justice, the prosecutor may not file an information until the defendant has had or waives a preliminary examination. An indictment is returned and filed without a preliminary examination. When this occurs, the indictment shall commence judicial proceedings.

(C) Time of Filing Information or Indictment. The prosecutor must file the information or indictment on or before the date set for the arraignment.

(D) Information; Nature and Contents; Attachments. The information must set forth the substance of the accusation against the defendant and the name, statutory citation, and penalty of the offense allegedly committed. If applicable, the information must also set forth the notice required by MCL 767.45, and the defendant's Michigan driver's license number. To the extent possible, the information should specify the time and place of the alleged offense. Allegations relating to conduct, the method of committing the offense, mental state, and the consequences of conduct may be stated in the alternative. A list of all witnesses known to the prosecutor who may be called at trial and all res gestae witnesses known to the prosecutor or investigating law enforcement officers must be attached to the information. A prosecutor must sign the information.

(E) Bill of Particulars. The court, on motion, may order the prosecutor to provide the defendant a bill of particulars describing the essential facts of the alleged offense.

(F) Notice of Intent to Seek Enhanced Sentence. A notice of intent to seek an enhanced sentence pursuant to MCL 769.13 must list the prior convictions that may be relied upon for purposes of sentence enhancement. The notice must be filed within 21 days after the defendant's arraignment on the information charging the underlying offense or, if arraignment is waived or eliminated as allowed under MCR 6.113(E), within 21 days after the filing of the information charging the underlying offense.

(G) Harmless Error. Absent a timely objection and a showing of prejudice, a court may not dismiss an information or reverse a conviction because of an untimely filing or because of an incorrectly cited statute or a variance between the information and proof regarding time, place, the manner in which the offense was committed, or other factual detail relating to the alleged offense.

(H) Amendment of Information or Notice of Intent to Seek Enhanced Sentence. The court before, during, or after trial may permit the prosecutor to amend the information or the notice of intent to seek enhanced sentence unless the proposed amendment would unfairly surprise or prejudice the defendant. On motion, the court must strike unnecessary allegations from the information.

Rule 6.113 The Arraignment on the Indictment or Information

(A) Time of Conducting. Unless the defendant waives arraignment or the court for good cause orders a delay, or as otherwise permitted by these rules, the court with trial jurisdiction must arraign the defendant on the scheduled date. The court may hold the arraignment before the preliminary examination transcript has been prepared and filed. Unless the defendant demonstrates actual prejudice, failure to hold the arraignment on the scheduled date is to be deemed harmless error.

(B) Arraignment Procedure. The prosecutor must give a copy of the information to the defendant before the defendant is asked to plead. Unless waived by the defendant, the court must either state to the defendant the substance of the charge contained in the information or require the information to be read to the defendant. If the defendant has waived legal representation, the court must advise the defendant of the pleading options. If the defendant offers a plea other than not guilty, the court must proceed in accordance with the rules in subchapter 6.300. Otherwise, the court must enter a plea of not guilty on the record. A verbatim record must be made of the arraignment.

(C) Waiver. A defendant represented by a lawyer may, as a matter of right, enter a plea of not guilty or stand mute without arraignment by filing, at or before the time set for the arraignment, a written statement signed by the defendant and the defendant's lawyer acknowledging that the defendant has received a copy of the information, has read or had it read or explained, understands the substance of the charge, waives arraignment in open court, and pleads not guilty to the charge or stands mute.

(D) Preliminary Examination Transcript. The court reporter shall transcribe and file the record of the preliminary examination if such is demanded or ordered pursuant to MCL 766.15.

(E) Elimination of Arraignments. A circuit court may submit to the State Court Administrator pursuant to MCR 8.112(B) a local administrative order that eliminates arraignment for a defendant represented by an attorney, provided other arrangements are made to give the defendant a copy of the information and any notice of intent to seek an enhanced sentence, as provided in MCR 6.112(F).

RULE 6.120 JOINDER AND SEVERANCE; SINGLE DEFENDANT

(A) Charging Joinder. The prosecuting attorney may file an information or indictment that charges a single defendant with any two or more offenses. Each offense must be stated in a separate count. Two or more informations or indictments against a single defendant may be consolidated for a single trial.

(B) Postcharging Permissive Joinder or Severance. On its own initiative, the motion of a party, or the stipulation of all parties, except as provided in subrule (C), the court may join offenses charged in two or more informations or indictments against a single defendant, or sever offenses charged in a single information or indictment against a single defendant, when appropriate to promote fairness to the parties and a fair determination of the defendant's guilt or innocence of each offense.

    (1) Joinder is appropriate if the offenses are related. For purposes of this rule, offenses are related if they are based on

        (a) the same conduct or transaction, or

        (b) a series of connected acts, or

        (c) a series of acts constituting parts of a single scheme or plan.

    (2) Other relevant factors include the timeliness of the motion, the drain on the parties' resources, the potential for confusion or prejudice stemming from either the number of charges or the complexity or nature of the evidence, the potential for harassment, the convenience of witnesses, and the parties' readiness for trial.

    (3) If the court acts on its own initiative, it must provide the parties an opportunity to be heard.

(C) Right of Severance; Unrelated Offenses. On the defendant's motion, the court must sever for separate trials offenses that are not related as defined in subrule (B)(1).

RULE 6.121 JOINDER AND SEVERANCE; MULTIPLE DEFENDANTS

(A) Permissive Joinder. An information or indictment may charge two or more defendants with the same offense. It may charge two or more defendants with two or more offenses when

    (1) each defendant is charged with accountability for each offense, or

(2) the offenses are related as defined in MCR 6.120(B).

When more than one offense is alleged, each offense must be stated in a separate count. Two or more informations or indictments against different defendants may be consolidated for a single trial whenever the defendants could be charged in the same information or indictment under this rule.

(B) Right of Severance; Unrelated Offenses. On a defendant's motion, the court must sever offenses that are not related as defined in MCR 6.120(B).

(C) Right of Severance; Related Offenses. On a defendant's motion, the court must sever the trial of defendants on related offenses on a showing that severance is necessary to avoid prejudice to substantial rights of the defendant.

(D) Discretionary Severance. On the motion of any party, the court may sever the trial of defendants on the ground that severance is appropriate to promote fairness to the parties and a fair determination of the guilt or innocence of one or more of the defendants. Relevant factors include the timeliness of the motion, the drain on the parties' resources, the potential for confusion or prejudice stemming from either the number of defendants or the complexity or nature of the evidence, the convenience of witnesses, and the parties' readiness for trial.

RULE 6.125 MENTAL COMPETENCY HEARING

(A) Applicable Provisions. Except as provided in these rules, a mental competency hearing in a criminal case is governed by MCL 330.2020 *et seq.*

(B) Time and Form of Motion. The issue of the defendant's competence to stand trial or to participate in other criminal proceedings may be raised at any time during the proceedings against the defendant. The issue may be raised by the court before which such proceedings are pending or being held, or by motion of a party. Unless the issue of defendant's competence arises during the course of proceedings, a motion raising the issue of defendant's competence must be in writing. If the competency issue arises during the course of proceedings, the court may adjourn the proceeding or, if the proceeding is defendant's trial, the court may, consonant with double jeopardy considerations, declare a mistrial.

(C) Order for Examination.

(1) On a showing that the defendant may be incompetent to stand trial, the court must order the defendant to undergo an examination by a certified or licensed examiner of the center for forensic psychiatry or other facility officially certified by the department of mental health to perform examinations relating to the issue of competence to stand trial.

(2) The defendant must appear for the examination as required by the court.

(3) If the defendant is held in detention pending trial, the examination may be performed in the place of detention or the defendant may be transported by the sheriff to the diagnostic facility for examination.

(4) The court may order commitment to a diagnostic facility for examination if the defendant fails to appear for the examination as required or if commitment is necessary for the performance of the examination.

(5) The defendant must be released from the facility on completion of the examination and, if (3) is applicable, returned to the place of detention.

(D) Independent Examination. On a showing of good cause by either party, the court may order an independent examination of the defendant relating to the issue of competence to stand trial.

(E) Hearing. A competency hearing must be held within 5 days of receipt of the report required by MCL 330.2028 or on conclusion of the proceedings then before the court, whichever is sooner, unless the court, on a showing of good cause, grants an adjournment.

(F) Motions; Testimony.

(1) A motion made while a defendant is incompetent to stand trial must be heard and decided if the presence of the defendant is not essential for a fair hearing and decision on the motion.

(2) Testimony may be presented on a pretrial defense motion if the defendant's presence could not assist the defense.

Subchapter 6.200 Discovery

Rule 6.201 Discovery

(A) Mandatory Disclosure. In addition to disclosures required by provisions of law other than MCL 767.94a, a party upon request must provide all other parties:

(1) the names and addresses of all lay and expert witnesses whom the party may call at trial; in the alternative, a party may provide the name of the witness and make the witness available to the other party for interview; the witness list may be amended without leave of the court no later than 28 days before trial;

(2) any written or recorded statement, including electronically recorded statements, pertaining to the case by a lay witness whom the party may call at trial, except that a defendant is not obliged to provide the defendant's own statement;

(3) the curriculum vitae of an expert the party may call at trial and either a report by the expert or a written description of the substance of the proposed testimony of the expert, the expert's opinion, and the underlying basis of that opinion;

(4) any criminal record that the party may use at trial to impeach a witness;

(5) a description or list of criminal convictions, known to the defense attorney or prosecuting attorney, of any witness whom the party may call at trial; and

(6) a description of and an opportunity to inspect any tangible physical evidence that the party may introduce at trial, including any document, photograph, or other paper, with copies to be provided on request. A party may request a hearing regarding any question of costs of reproduction, including the cost of providing copies of electronically recorded statements. On good cause shown, the court may order that a party be given the opportunity to test without destruction any tangible physical evidence.

(B) Discovery of Information Known to the Prosecuting Attorney. Upon request, the prosecuting attorney must provide each defendant:

(1) any exculpatory information or evidence known to the prosecuting attorney;

(2) any police report and interrogation records concerning the case, except so much of a report as concerns a continuing investigation;

(3) any written or recorded statements, including electronically recorded statements, by a defendant, codefendant, or accomplice pertaining to the case, even if that person is not a prospective witness at trial;

(4) any affidavit, warrant, and return pertaining to a search or seizure in connection with the case; and

(5) any plea agreement, grant of immunity, or other agreement for testimony in connection with the case.

(C) Prohibited Discovery.

(1) Notwithstanding any other provision of this rule, there is no right to discover information or evidence that is protected from disclosure by constitution, statute, or privilege, including information or evidence protected by a defendant's right against self-incrimination, except as provided in subrule (2).

(2) If a defendant demonstrates a good-faith belief, grounded in articulable fact, that there is a reasonable probability that records protected by privilege are likely to contain material information necessary to the defense, the trial court shall conduct an in camera inspection of the records.

(a) If the privilege is absolute, and the privilege holder refuses to waive the privilege to permit an in camera inspection, the trial court shall suppress or strike the privilege holder's testimony.

(b) If the court is satisfied, following an in camera inspection, that the records reveal evidence necessary to the defense, the court shall direct that such evidence as is necessary to the defense be made available to defense counsel. If the privilege is absolute and the privilege holder refuses to waive the privilege to permit disclosure, the trial court shall suppress or strike the privilege holder's testimony.

(c) Regardless of whether the court determines that the records should be made available to the defense, the court shall make findings sufficient to facilitate meaningful appellate review.

(d) The court shall seal and preserve the records for review in the event of an appeal

(i) by the defendant, on an interlocutory basis or following conviction, if the court determines that the records should not be made available to the defense, or

(ii) by the prosecution, on an interlocutory basis, if the court determines that the records should be made available to the defense.

(e) Records disclosed under this rule shall remain in the exclusive custody of counsel for the parties, shall be used only for the limited purpose approved by the court, and shall be subject to such other terms and conditions as the court may provide.

(D) Excision. When some parts of material or information are discoverable and other parts are not discoverable, the party must disclose the discoverable parts and may excise the remainder. The party must inform the other party that nondiscoverable information has been excised and withheld. On motion, the court must conduct a hearing in camera to determine whether the reasons for excision are justifiable. If the court upholds the excision, it must seal and preserve the record of the hearing for review in the event of an appeal.

(E) Protective Orders. On motion and a showing of good cause, the court may enter an appropriate protective order. In considering whether good cause exists, the court shall consider the parties' interests in a fair trial; the risk to any person of harm, undue annoyance, intimidation, embarrassment, or threats; the risk that evidence will be fabricated; and the need for secrecy regarding the identity of informants or other law enforcement matters. On motion, with notice to the other party, the court may permit the showing of good cause for a protective order to be made in camera. If the court grants a protective order, it must seal and preserve the record of the hearing for review in the event of an appeal.

(F) Timing of Discovery. Unless otherwise ordered by the court, the prosecuting attorney must comply with the requirements of this rule within 21 days of a request under this rule and a defendant must comply with the requirements of this rule within 21 days of a request under this rule.

(G) Copies. Except as ordered by the court on good cause shown, a party's obligation to provide a photograph or paper of any kind is satisfied by providing a clear copy.

(H) Continuing Duty to Disclose. If at any time a party discovers additional information or material subject to disclosure under this rule, the party, without further request, must promptly notify the other party.

(I) Modification. On good cause shown, the court may order a modification of the requirements and prohibitions of this rule.

(J) Violation. If a party fails to comply with this rule, the court, in its discretion, may order the party to provide the discovery or permit the inspection of materials not previously disclosed, grant a continuance, prohibit the party from introducing in evidence the material not disclosed, or enter such other order as it deems just under the circumstances. Parties are encouraged to bring questions of noncompliance before the court at the earliest opportunity. Willful violation by counsel of an applicable discovery rule or an order issued pursuant thereto may subject counsel to appropriate sanctions by the court. An order of the court under this section is reviewable only for abuse of discretion.

(K) Except as otherwise provided in MCR 2.302(B)(6), electronic materials are to be treated in the same manner as nonelectronic materials under this rule. Nothing in this rule shall be construed to conflict with MCL 600.2163a.

RULE 6.202. DISCLOSURE OF FORENSIC LABORATORY REPORT AND CERTIFICATE; APPLICABILITY; ADMISSIBILITY OF REPORT AND CERTIFICATE; EXTENSION OF TIME; ADJOURNMENT

(A) This rule shall apply to criminal trials in the district and circuit courts.

(B) Disclosure. Upon receipt of a forensic laboratory report and certificate, if applicable, by the examining expert, the prosecutor shall serve a copy of the laboratory report and certificate on the opposing party's attorney or party, if not represented by an attorney, within 14 days after receipt of the laboratory report and certificate. A proof of service of the report and certificate, if applicable, on the opposing party's attorney or party, if not represented by an attorney, shall be filed with the court.

(C) Notice and Demand.

(1) Notice. If a party intends to offer the report described in subsection (B) as evidence at trial, the party's attorney or party, if not represented by an attorney, shall provide the opposing party's attorney or party, if not represented by an attorney, with notice of that fact in writing. If the prosecuting attorney intends to offer the report as evidence at trial, notice to the defendant's attorney or the defendant, if not

represented by an attorney, shall be included with the report. If the defendant intends to offer the report as evidence at trial, notice to the prosecuting attorney shall be provided within 14 days after receipt of the report. Except as provided in subrule (C)(2), the report and certification, if applicable, is admissible in evidence to the same effect as if the person who performed the analysis or examination had personally testified.

(2) Demand. Upon receipt of a copy of the laboratory report and certificate, if applicable, the opposing party's attorney or party, if not represented by an attorney, may file a written objection to the use of the laboratory report and certificate. The written objection shall be filed with the court in which the matter is pending, and shall be served on the opposing party's attorney or party, if not represented by an attorney, within 14 days of receipt of the notice. If a written objection is filed, the report and certificate are not admissible under subrule (C)(1). If no objection is made to the use of the laboratory report and certificate within the time allowed by this section, the report and certificate are admissible in evidence as provided in subrule (C)(1).

(3) For good cause the court shall extend the time period of filing a written objection.

(4) Adjournment. Compliance with this court rule shall be good cause for an adjournment of the trial.

(D) Certification. Except as otherwise provided, the analyst who conducts the analysis on the forensic sample and signs the report shall complete a certificate on which the analyst shall state (i) that he or she is qualified by education, training, and experience to perform the analysis, (ii) the name and location of the laboratory where the analysis was performed, (iii) that performing the analysis is part of his or her regular duties, and (iv) that the tests were performed under industry-approved procedures or standards and the report accurately reflects the analyst's findings and opinions regarding the results of those tests or analysis. A report submitted by an analyst who is employed by a laboratory that is accredited by a national or international accreditation entity that substantially meets the certification requirements described above may provide proof of the laboratory's accreditation certificate in lieu of a separate certificate.

Subchapter 6.300 Pleas

Rule 6.301 Available Pleas

(A) Possible Pleas. Subject to the rules in this subchapter, a defendant may plead not guilty, guilty, nolo contendere, guilty but mentally ill, or not guilty by reason of insanity. If the defendant refuses to plead or stands mute, or the court, pursuant to the rules, refuses to accept the defendant's plea, the court must enter a not guilty plea on the record. A plea of not guilty places in issue every material allegation in the information and permits the defendant to raise any defense not otherwise waived.

(B) Pleas That Require the Court's Consent. A defendant may enter a plea of nolo contendere only with the consent of the court.

(C) Pleas That Require the Consent of the Court and the Prosecutor. A defendant may enter the following pleas only with the consent of the court and the prosecutor:

(1) A defendant who has asserted an insanity defense may enter a plea of guilty but mentally ill or a plea of not guilty by reason of insanity. Before such a plea may be entered, the defendant must comply with the examination required by law.

(2) A defendant may enter a conditional plea of guilty, nolo contendere, guilty but mentally ill, or not guilty by reason of insanity. A conditional plea preserves for appeal a specified pretrial ruling or rulings notwithstanding the plea-based judgment and entitles the defendant to withdraw the plea if a specified pretrial ruling is overturned on appeal. The ruling or rulings as to which the defendant reserves the right to appeal must be specified orally on the record or in a writing made a part of the record. The appeal is by application for leave to appeal only.

(D) Pleas to Lesser Charges. The court may not accept a plea to an offense other than the one charged without the consent of the prosecutor.

RULE 6.302 PLEAS OF GUILTY AND NOLO CONTENDERE

(A) Plea Requirements. The court may not accept a plea of guilty or nolo contendere unless it is convinced that the plea is understanding, voluntary, and accurate. Before accepting a plea of guilty or nolo contendere, the court must place the defendant or defendants under oath and personally carry out subrules (B)-(E).

(B) An Understanding Plea. Speaking directly to the defendant or defendants, the court must advise the defendant or defendants of the following and determine that each defendant understands:

(1) the name of the offense to which the defendant is pleading; the court is not obliged to explain the elements of the offense, or possible defenses;

(2) the maximum possible prison sentence for the offense and any mandatory minimum sentence required by law, including a requirement for mandatory lifetime electronic monitoring under MCL 750.520b or 750.520c;

(3) if the plea is accepted, the defendant will not have a trial of any kind, and so gives up the rights the defendant would have at a trial, including the right:

(a) to be tried by a jury;

(b) to be presumed innocent until proved guilty;

(c) to have the prosecutor prove beyond a reasonable doubt that the defendant is guilty;

(d) to have the witnesses against the defendant appear at the trial;

(e) to question the witnesses against the defendant;

(f) to have the court order any witnesses the defendant has for the defense to appear at the trial;

(g) to remain silent during the trial;

(h) to not have that silence used against the defendant; and

(i) to testify at the trial if the defendant wants to testify.

(4) if the plea is accepted, the defendant will be giving up any claim that the plea was the result of promises or threats that were not disclosed to the court at the plea proceeding, or that it was not the defendant's own choice to enter the plea;

(5) if the plea is accepted, the defendant may be giving up the right to appeal issues that would otherwise be appealable if she or he were convicted at trial. Further, any appeal from the conviction and sentence pursuant to the plea will be by application for leave to appeal and not by right;

The requirements of subrules (B)(3) and (B)(5) may be satisfied by a writing on a form approved by the State Court Administrative Office. If a court uses a writing, the court shall address the defendant and obtain from the defendant orally on the record a statement that the rights were read and understood and a waiver of those rights. The waiver may be obtained without repeating the individual rights.

(C) A Voluntary Plea.

(1) The court must ask the prosecutor and the defendant's lawyer whether they have made a plea agreement. If they have made a plea agreement, which may include an agreement to a sentence to a specific term or within a specific range, the agreement must be stated on the record or reduced to writing and signed by the parties. The parties may memorialize their agreement on a form substantially approved by the SCAO. The written agreement shall be made part of the case file.

(2) If there is a plea agreement, the court must ask the prosecutor or the defendant's lawyer what the terms of the agreement are and confirm the terms of the agreement with the other lawyer and the defendant.

(3) If there is a plea agreement and its terms provide for the defendant's plea to be made in exchange for a sentence to a specified term or within a specified range or a prosecutorial sentence recommendation, the court may

(a) reject the agreement; or

(b) accept the agreement after having considered the presentence report, in which event it must sentence the defendant to a specified term or within a specified range as agreed to; or

(c) accept the agreement without having considered the presentence report; or

(d) take the plea agreement under advisement.

If the court accepts the agreement without having considered the presentence report or takes the plea agreement under advisement, it must explain to the defendant that the court is not bound to follow an agreement to a sentence for a specified term or within a specified range or a recommendation agreed to by the prosecutor, and that if the court chooses not to follow an agreement to a sentence for a specified term or within a specified range, the defendant will be allowed to withdraw from the plea agreement. A judge's decision not to follow the sentence recommendation does not entitle the defendant to withdraw the defendant's plea.

(4) The court must ask the defendant:

(a) (if there is no plea agreement) whether anyone has promised the defendant anything, or (if there is a plea agreement) whether anyone has promised anything beyond what is in the plea agreement;

(b) whether anyone has threatened the defendant; and

(c) whether it is the defendant's own choice to plead guilty.

(D) An Accurate Plea.

(1) If the defendant pleads guilty, the court, by questioning the defendant, must establish support for a finding that the defendant is guilty of the offense charged or the offense to which the defendant is pleading.

(2) If the defendant pleads nolo contendere, the court may not question the defendant about participation in the crime. The court must:

(a) state why a plea of nolo contendere is appropriate; and

(b) hold a hearing, unless there has been one, that establishes support for a finding that the defendant is guilty of the offense charged or the offense to which the defendant is pleading.

(E) Additional Inquiries. On completing the colloquy with the defendant, the court must ask the prosecutor and the defendant's lawyer whether either is aware of any promises, threats, or inducements other than those already disclosed on the record, and whether the court has complied with subrules (B)-(D). If it appears to the court that it has failed to comply with subrules (B)-(D), the court may not accept the defendant's plea until the deficiency is corrected.

(F) Plea Under Advisement; Plea Record. The court may take the plea under advisement. A verbatim record must be made of the plea proceeding.

RULE 6.303 PLEA OF GUILTY BUT MENTALLY ILL

Before accepting a plea of guilty but mentally ill, the court must comply with the requirements of MCR 6.302. In addition to establishing a factual basis for the plea pursuant to MCR 6.302(D)(1) or (D)(2)(b), the court must examine the psychiatric reports prepared and hold a hearing that establishes support for a finding that the defendant was mentally ill, at the time of the offense to which the plea is entered. The reports must be made a part of the record.

RULE 6.304 PLEA OF NOT GUILTY BY REASON OF INSANITY

(A) Advice to Defendant. Before accepting a plea of not guilty by reason of insanity, the court must comply with the requirements of MCR 6.302 except that subrule (C) of this rule, rather than MCR 6.302(D), governs the manner of determining the accuracy of the plea.

(B) Additional Advice Required. After complying with the applicable requirements of MCR 6.302, the court must advise the defendant, and determine whether the defendant understands, that the plea will result in the defendant's commitment for diagnostic examination at the center for forensic psychiatry for up to 60 days, and that after the examination, the probate court may order the defendant to be committed for an indefinite period of time.

(C) Factual Basis. Before accepting a plea of not guilty by reason of insanity, the court must examine the psychiatric reports prepared and hold a hearing that establishes support for findings that

(1) the defendant committed the acts charged, and

(2) that, by a preponderance of the evidence, the defendant was legally insane at the time of the offense.

(D) Report of Plea. After accepting the defendant's plea, the court must forward to the center for forensic psychiatry a full report, in the form of a settled record, of the facts concerning the crime to which the defendant pleaded and the defendant's mental state at the time of the crime.

RULE 6.310 WITHDRAWAL OR VACATION OF PLEA

(A) Withdrawal Before Acceptance. The defendant has a right to withdraw any plea until the court accepts it on the record.

(B) Withdrawal After Acceptance but Before Sentence. Except as provided in subsection (3), after acceptance but before sentence,

(1) a plea may be withdrawn on the defendant's motion or with the defendant's consent, only in the interest of justice, and may not be withdrawn if withdrawal of the plea would substantially prejudice the prosecutor because of reliance on the plea. If the defendant's motion is based on an error in the plea proceeding, the court must permit the defendant to withdraw the plea if it would be required by subrule (C).

(2) the defendant is entitled to withdraw the plea if

(a) the plea involves an agreement for a sentence for a specified term or within a specified range, and the court states that it is unable to follow the agreement; the trial court shall then state the sentence it intends to impose, and provide the defendant the opportunity to affirm or withdraw the plea; or

(b) the plea involves a statement by the court that it will sentence to a specified term or within a specified range, and the court states that it is unable to sentence as stated; the trial court shall provide the defendant the opportunity to affirm or withdraw the plea, but shall not state the sentence it intends to impose.

(3) Except as allowed by the trial court for good cause, a defendant is not entitled to withdraw a plea under subsection (2)(a) or (2)(b) if the defendant commits misconduct after the plea is accepted but before sentencing. For purposes of this rule, misconduct is defined to include, but is not limited to: absconding or failing to appear for sentencing, violating terms of conditions on bond or the terms of any sentencing or plea agreement, or otherwise failing to comply with an order of the court pending sentencing.

(C) Motion to Withdraw Plea After Sentence.

(1) The defendant may file a motion to withdraw the plea within 6 months after sentence or within the time provided by subrule (C)(2).

(2) If 6 months have elapsed since sentencing, the defendant may file a motion to withdraw the plea if:

(a) the defendant has filed a request for the appointment of counsel pursuant to MCR 6.425(G)(1) within the 6-month period,

(b) the defendant or defendant's lawyer, if one is appointed, has ordered the appropriate transcripts within 28 days of service of the order granting or denying the request for counsel or substitute counsel, unless the transcript has already been filed or has been ordered by the court under MCR 6.425(G), and

(c) the motion to withdraw the plea is filed in accordance with the provisions of this subrule within 42 days after the filing of the transcript. If the transcript was filed before the order appointing counsel or substitute counsel, or the order denying the appointment of counsel, the 42-day period runs from the date of that order.

(3) Thereafter, the defendant may seek relief only in accordance with the procedure set forth in subchapter 6.500.

(4) If the trial court determines that there was an error in the plea proceeding that would entitle the defendant to have the plea set aside, the court must give the advice or make the inquiries necessary to rectify the error and then give the defendant the opportunity to elect to allow the plea and sentence to stand or to withdraw the plea. If the defendant elects to allow the plea and sentence to stand, the additional advice given and inquiries made become part of the plea proceeding for the purposes of further proceedings, including appeals.

(5) If a motion to withdraw plea is received by the court after the expiration of the periods set forth above, and if the appellant is an inmate in the custody of the Michigan Department of Corrections and has submitted the motion as a pro se party, the motion shall be deemed presented for filing on the date of deposit of the motion in the outgoing mail at the correctional institution in which the inmate is housed. Timely filing may be shown by a sworn statement filed with the motion, which must set forth the date of deposit and state that first-class postage has been prepaid. The exception applies to cases

in which a plea was accepted on or after the effective date of this amendment. This exception also applies to an inmate housed in a penal institution in another state or in a federal penal institution who seeks to withdraw a plea in a Michigan court.

(D) Preservation of Issues. A defendant convicted on the basis of a plea may not raise on appeal any claim of noncompliance with the requirements of the rules in this subchapter, or any other claim that the plea was not an understanding, voluntary, or accurate one, unless the defendant has moved to withdraw the plea in the trial court, raising as a basis for withdrawal the claim sought to be raised on appeal.

(E) Vacation of Plea on Prosecutor's Motion. On the prosecutor's motion, the court may vacate a plea if the defendant has failed to comply with the terms of a plea agreement.

Rule 6.312 Effect of Withdrawal or Vacation of Plea

If a plea is withdrawn by the defendant or vacated by the trial court or an appellate court, the case may proceed to trial on any charges that had been brought or that could have been brought against the defendant if the plea had not been entered.

Subchapter 6.400 Trials

Rule 6.401 Right to Trial by Jury or by the Court

The defendant has the right to be tried by a jury, or may, with the consent of the prosecutor and approval by the court, elect to waive that right and be tried before the court without a jury.

Rule 6.402 Waiver of Jury Trial by the Defendant

(A) Time of Waiver. The court may not accept a waiver of trial by jury until after the defendant has been arraigned or has waived an arraignment on the information, or, in a court where arraignment on the information has been eliminated under MCR 6.113(E), after the defendant has otherwise been provided with a copy of the information, and has been offered an opportunity to consult with a lawyer.

(B) Waiver and Record Requirements. Before accepting a waiver, the court must advise the defendant in open court of the constitutional right to trial by jury. The court must also ascertain, by addressing the defendant personally, that the defendant understands the right and that the defendant voluntarily chooses to give up that right and to be tried by the court. A verbatim record must be made of the waiver proceeding.

Rule 6.403 Trial by the Judge in Waiver Cases

When trial by jury has been waived, the court with jurisdiction must proceed with the trial. The court must find the facts specially, state separately its conclusions of law, and direct entry of the appropriate judgment. The court must state its findings and conclusions on the record or in a written opinion made a part of the record.

Rule 6.410 Jury Trial; Number of Jurors; Unanimous Verdict

(A) Number of Jurors. Except as provided in this rule, a jury that decides a case must consist of 12 jurors. At any time before a verdict is returned, the parties may stipulate with the court's consent to have the case decided by a jury consisting of a specified number of jurors less than 12. On being informed of the parties' willingness to stipulate, the court must personally advise the defendant of the right to have the case decided by a jury consisting of 12 jurors. By addressing the defendant personally, the court must ascertain that the defendant understands the right and that the defendant voluntarily chooses to give up that right as provided in the stipulation. If the court finds that the requirements for a valid waiver have been satisfied, the court may accept the stipulation. Even if the requirements for a valid waiver have been satisfied, the court may, in the interest of justice, refuse to accept a stipulation, but it must state its reasons for doing so on the record. The stipulation and procedure described in this subrule must take place in open court and a verbatim record must be made.

(B) Unanimous Verdicts. A jury verdict must be unanimous.

RULE 6.411 ADDITIONAL JURORS

The court may impanel more than 12 jurors. If more than the number of jurors required to decide the case are left on the jury before deliberations are to begin, the names of the jurors must be placed in a container and names drawn from it to reduce the number of jurors to the number required to decide the case. The court may retain the alternate jurors during deliberations. If the court does so, it shall instruct the alternate jurors not to discuss the case with any other person until the jury completes its deliberations and is discharged. If an alternate juror replaces a juror after the jury retires to consider its verdict, the court shall instruct the jury to begin its deliberations anew.

RULE 6.412 SELECTION OF THE JURY

(A) Selecting and Impaneling the Jury. Except as otherwise provided by the rules in this subchapter, MCR 2.510 and 2.511 govern the procedure for selecting and impaneling the jury.

(B) Instructions and Oath Before Selection. Before beginning the jury selection process, the court should give the prospective jurors appropriate preliminary instructions and must have them sworn.

(C) Voir Dire of Prospective Jurors.

(1) Scope and Purpose. The scope of voir dire examination of prospective jurors is within the discretion of the court. It should be conducted for the purposes of discovering grounds for challenges for cause and of gaining knowledge to facilitate an intelligent exercise of peremptory challenges. The court should confine the examination to these purposes and prevent abuse of the examination process.

(2) Conduct of the Examination. The court may conduct the examination of prospective jurors or permit the lawyers to do so. If the court conducts the examination, it may permit the lawyers to supplement the examination by direct questioning or by submitting questions for the court to ask. On its own initiative or on the motion of a party, the court may provide for a prospective juror or jurors to be questioned out of the presence of the other jurors.

(D) Challenges for Cause.

(1) Grounds. A prospective juror is subject to challenge for cause on any ground set forth in MCR 2.511(D) or for any other reason recognized by law.

(2) Procedure. If, after the examination of any juror, the court finds that a ground for challenging a juror for cause is present, the court on its own initiative should, or on motion of either party must, excuse the juror from the panel.

(E) Peremptory Challenges.

(1) Challenges by Right. Each defendant is entitled to 5 peremptory challenges unless an offense charged is punishable by life imprisonment, in which case a defendant

being tried alone is entitled to 12 peremptory challenges, 2 defendants being tried jointly are each entitled to 10 peremptory challenges, 3 defendants being tried jointly are each entitled to 9 peremptory challenges, 4 defendants being tried jointly are each entitled to 8 peremptory challenges, and 5 or more defendants being tried jointly are each entitled to 7 peremptory challenges. The prosecutor is entitled to the same number of peremptory challenges as a defendant being tried alone, or, in the case of jointly tried defendants, the total number of peremptory challenges to which all the defendants are entitled.

(2) Additional Challenges. On a showing of good cause, the court may grant one or more of the parties an increased number of peremptory challenges. The additional challenges granted by the court need not be equal for each party.

(F) Oath After Selection. After the jury is selected and before trial begins, the court must have the jurors sworn.

RULE 6.416 PRESENTATION OF EVIDENCE

Subject to the rules in this chapter and to the Michigan rules of evidence, each party has discretion in deciding what witnesses and evidence to present.

RULE 6.417 MISTRIAL

Before ordering a mistrial, the court must, on the record, give each defendant and the prosecutor an opportunity to comment on the propriety of the order, to state whether that party consents or objects, and to suggest alternatives.

RULE 6.419 MOTION FOR DIRECTED VERDICT OF ACQUITTAL

(A) Before Submission to the Jury. After the prosecutor has rested the prosecution's case-in-chief or after the close of all the evidence, the court on the defendant's motion must direct a verdict of acquittal on any charged offense for which the evidence is insufficient to sustain a conviction. The court may on its own consider whether the evidence is insufficient to sustain a conviction. If the court denies a motion for a judgment of acquittal at the close of the government's evidence, the defendant may offer evidence without having reserved the right to do so.

(B) Reserving Decision. The court may reserve decision on the motion, proceed with the trial (where the motion is made before the close of all the evidence), submit the case to the jury, and decide the motion either before the jury returns a verdict or after it returns a verdict of guilty or is discharged without having returned a verdict. If the court reserves decision, it must decide the motion on the basis of the evidence at the time the ruling was reserved.

(C) After Jury Verdict. After a jury verdict, the defendant may file an original or renewed motion for directed verdict of acquittal in the same manner as provided by MCR 6.431(A) for filing a motion for a new trial.

(D) Bench Trial. In an action tried without a jury, after the prosecutor has rested the prosecution's case-in-chief, the defendant, without waiving the right to offer evidence if the motion is not granted, may move for acquittal on the ground that a reasonable doubt exists. The court may then determine the facts and render a verdict of acquittal, or may decline to render judgment until the close of all the evidence. If the court renders a verdict of acquittal, the court shall make findings of fact.

(E) Conditional New Trial Ruling. If the court grants a directed verdict of acquittal after the jury has returned a guilty verdict, it must also conditionally rule on any motion for a new trial by determining whether it would grant the motion if the directed verdict of acquittal is vacated or reversed.

(F) Explanation of Rulings on Record. The court must state orally on the record or in a written ruling made a part of the record its reasons for granting or denying a motion for a directed verdict of acquittal and for conditionally granting or denying a motion for a new trial.

RULE 6.420 VERDICT

(A) Return. The jury must return its verdict in open court.

(B) Several Defendants. If two or more defendants are jointly on trial, the jury at any time during its deliberations may return a verdict with respect to any defendant as to whom it has agreed. If the jury cannot reach a verdict with respect to any other defendant, the court may declare a mistrial as to that defendant.

(C) Several Counts. If a defendant is charged with two or more counts, and the court determines that the jury is deadlocked so that a mistrial must be declared, the court may inquire of the jury whether it has reached a unanimous verdict on any of the counts charged, and, if so, may accept the jury's verdict on that count or counts.

(D) Poll of Jury. Before the jury is discharged, the court on its own initiative may, or on the motion of a party must, have each juror polled in open court as to whether the verdict announced is that juror's verdict. If polling discloses the jurors are not in agreement, the court may (1) discontinue the poll and order the jury to retire for further deliberations, or (2) either (a) with the defendant's consent, or (b) after determining that the jury is deadlocked or that some other manifest necessity exists, declare a mistrial and discharge the jury.

RULE 6.425 SENTENCING; APPOINTMENT OF APPELLATE COUNSEL

(A) Presentence Report; Contents.

    (1) Prior to sentencing, the probation officer must investigate the defendant's background and character, verify material information, and report in writing the results of the investigation to the court. The report must be succinct and, depending on the circumstances, include:

        (a) a description of the defendant's prior criminal convictions and juvenile adjudications,

        (b) a complete description of the offense and the circumstances surrounding it,

        (c) a brief description of the defendant's vocational background and work history, including military record and present employment status,

        (d) a brief social history of the defendant, including marital status, financial status, length of residence in the community, educational background, and other pertinent data,

        (e) the defendant's medical history, substance abuse history, if any, and, if indicated, a current psychological or psychiatric report,

        (f) information concerning the financial, social, psychological, or physical harm suffered by any victim of the offense, including the restitution needs of the victim,

        (g) if provided and requested by the victim, a written victim's impact statement as provided by law,

(h) any statement the defendant wishes to make,

(i) a statement prepared by the prosecutor on the applicability of any consecutive sentencing provision,

(j) an evaluation of and prognosis for the defendant's adjustment in the community based on factual information in the report,

(k) a specific recommendation for disposition, and

(l) any other information that may aid the court in sentencing.

(2) A presentence investigation report shall not include any address or telephone number for the home, workplace, school, or place of worship of any victim or witness, or a family member of any victim or witness, unless an address is used to identify the place of the crime or to impose conditions of release from custody that are necessary for the protection of a named individual. Upon request, any other address or telephone number that would reveal the location of a victim or witness or a family member of a victim or witness shall be exempted from disclosure unless an address is used to identify the place of the crime or to impose conditions of release from custody that are necessary for the protection of a named individual.

(3) Regardless of the sentence imposed, the court must have a copy of the presentence report and of any psychiatric report sent to the Department of Corrections. If the defendant is sentenced to prison, the copies must be sent with the commitment papers.

(B) Presentence Report; Disclosure Before Sentencing. The court must provide copies of the presentence report to the prosecutor, and the defendant's lawyer, or the defendant if not represented by a lawyer, at a reasonable time, but not less than two business days, before the day of sentencing. The prosecutor and the defendant's lawyer, or the defendant if not represented by a lawyer, may retain a copy of the report or an amended report. If the presentence report is not made available to the prosecutor and the defendant's lawyer, or the defendant if not represented by a lawyer, at least two business days before the day of sentencing, the prosecutor and the defendant's lawyer, or the defendant if not represented by a lawyer, shall be entitled, on oral motion, to an adjournment of the day of sentencing to enable the moving party to review the presentence report and to prepare any necessary corrections, additions, or deletions to present to the court. The court may exempt from disclosure information or diagnostic opinion that might seriously disrupt a program of rehabilitation and sources of information that have been obtained on a promise of confidentiality. When part of the report is not disclosed, the court must inform the parties that information has not been disclosed and state on the record the reasons for nondisclosure. To the extent it can do so without defeating the purpose of nondisclosure, the court also must provide the parties with a written or oral summary of the nondisclosed information and give them an opportunity to comment on it. The court must have the information exempted from disclosure specifically noted in the report. The court's decision to exempt part of the report from disclosure is subject to appellate review.

(C) Presentence Report; Disclosure After Sentencing. After sentencing, the court, on written request, must provide the prosecutor, the defendant's lawyer, or the defendant not represented by a lawyer, with a copy of the presentence report and any attachments to it. The court must exempt from disclosure any information the sentencing court exempted from disclosure pursuant to subrule (B).

(D) Sentencing Guidelines. The court must use the sentencing guidelines, as provided by law. Proposed scoring of the guidelines shall accompany the presentence report.

(E) Sentencing Procedure.

(1) The court must sentence the defendant within a reasonably prompt time after the plea or verdict unless the court delays sentencing as provided by law. At sentencing, the court must, on the record:

(a) determine that the defendant, the defendant's lawyer, and the prosecutor have had an opportunity to read and discuss the presentence report,

(b) give each party an opportunity to explain, or challenge the accuracy or relevancy of, any information in the presentence report, and resolve any challenges in accordance with the procedure set forth in subrule (E)(2),

(c) give the defendant, the defendant's lawyer, the prosecutor, and the victim an opportunity to advise the court of any circumstances they believe the court should consider in imposing sentence,

(d) state the sentence being imposed, including the minimum and maximum sentence if applicable, together with any credit for time served to which the defendant is entitled,

(e) if the sentence imposed is not within the guidelines range, articulate the reasons justifying that specific departure, and

(f) order the dollar amount of restitution that the defendant must pay to make full restitution as required by law to any victim of the defendant's course of conduct that gives rise to the conviction, or to that victim's estate.

(2) Resolution of Challenges.

(a) If any information in the presentence report is challenged, the court must allow the parties to be heard regarding the challenge, and make a finding with respect to the challenge or determine that a finding is unnecessary because it will not take the challenged information into account in sentencing. If the court finds merit in the challenge or determines that it will not take the challenged information into account in sentencing, it must direct the probation officer to

(i) correct or delete the challenged information in the report, whichever is appropriate, and

(ii) provide defendant's lawyer with an opportunity to review the corrected report before it is sent to the Department of Corrections.

(b) Any dispute as to the proper amount or type of restitution shall be resolved by the court by a preponderance of the evidence. The burden of demonstrating the amount of the loss sustained by a victim as a result of the offense shall be on the prosecuting attorney.

(3) Incarceration for Nonpayment.

(a) The court shall not sentence a defendant to a term of incarceration, nor revoke probation, for failure to comply with an order to pay money unless the court finds, on the record, that the defendant is able to comply with the order without manifest hardship and that the defendant has not made a good-faith effort to comply with the order.

(b) Payment alternatives. If the court finds that the defendant is unable to comply with an order to pay money without manifest hardship, the court may impose a payment alternative, such as a payment plan, modification of any existing payment plan, or waiver of part or all of the amount of money owed to the extent permitted by law.

(c) Determining manifest hardship. The court shall consider the following criteria in determining manifest hardship:

 (i) Defendant's employment status and history.

 (ii) Defendant's employability and earning ability.

 (iii) The willfulness of the defendant's failure to pay.

 (iv) Defendant's financial resources.

 (v) Defendant's basic living expenses including but not limited to food, shelter, clothing, necessary medical expenses, or child support.

 (vi) Any other special circumstances that may have bearing on the defendant's ability to pay.

(F) Advice Concerning the Right to Appeal; Appointment of Counsel.

(1) In a case involving a conviction following a trial, immediately after imposing sentence, the court must advise the defendant, on the record, that

 (a) the defendant is entitled to appellate review of the conviction and sentence,

 (b) if the defendant is financially unable to retain a lawyer, the court will appoint a lawyer to represent the defendant on appeal, and

 (c) the request for a lawyer must be filed within 42 days after sentencing.

(2) In a case involving a conviction following a plea of guilty or nolo contendere, immediately after imposing sentence, the court must advise the defendant, on the record, that

 (a) the defendant is entitled to file an application for leave to appeal,

 (b) if the defendant is financially unable to retain a lawyer, the court will appoint a lawyer to represent the defendant on appeal, and

 (c) the request for a lawyer must be filed within 42 days after sentencing.

(3) The court also must give the defendant a request for counsel form containing an instruction informing the defendant that the form must be completed and filed within 42 days after sentencing if the defendant wants the court to appoint a lawyer. The court must give the defendant an opportunity to tender a completed request for counsel form at sentencing if the defendant wishes to do so.

(4) A request for counsel must be deemed filed on the date on which it is received by the court or the Michigan Appellate Assigned Counsel System (MAACS), whichever is earlier.

(5) When imposing sentence in a case in which sentencing guidelines enacted in 1998 PA 317, MCL 777.1 *et seq.,* are applicable, if the court imposes a minimum sentence that is longer or more severe than the range provided by the sentencing guidelines, the court must advise the defendant on the record and in writing that the defendant may seek appellate review of the sentence, by right if the conviction followed trial or by application if the conviction entered by plea, on the ground that it is longer or more severe than the range provided by the sentencing guidelines.

(G) Appointment of Lawyer and Preparation of Transcript; Scope of Appellate Lawyer's Responsibilities.

(1) Appointment of Lawyer and Preparation of Transcript.

 (a) All requests for the appointment of appellate counsel must be granted or denied on forms approved by the State Court Administrative Office and provided by MAACS.

 (b) Within 7 days after receiving a defendant's request for a lawyer, or within 7 days after the disposition of a postjudgment motion if one is filed, the trial court must submit the request, the judgment of sentence, the register of actions, and any additional requested information to MAACS under procedures approved by the Appellate Defender Commission for the preparation of an appropriate order granting or denying the request. The court must notify MAACS if it intends to deny the request for counsel.

(c) Within 7 days after receiving a request and related information from the trial court, MAACS must provide the court with a proposed order appointing appellate counsel or denying the appointment of appellate counsel. A proposed appointment order must name the State Appellate Defender Office (SADO) or an approved private attorney who is willing to accept an appointment for the appeal.

(d) Within 7 days after receiving a proposed order from MAACS, the trial court must rule on the request for a lawyer. If the defendant is indigent, the court must enter an order appointing a lawyer if the request for a lawyer is filed within 42 days after entry of the judgment of sentence or, if applicable, within the time for filing an appeal of right. The court should liberally grant an untimely request as long as the defendant may file an application for leave to appeal. An order denying a request for the appointment of appellate counsel must include a statement of reasons and must inform the defendant that the order denying the request may be appealed by filing an application for leave to appeal in the Court of Appeals in accordance with MCR 7.205.

(e) In a case involving a conviction following a trial, if the defendant's request for a lawyer was filed within the time for filing a claim of appeal, the order must be entered on an approved form entitled "Claim of Appeal and Appointment of Counsel." Entry of the order by the trial court pursuant to this subrule constitutes a timely filed claim of appeal for the purposes of MCR 7.204.

(f) An appointment order must direct the court reporter to prepare and file, within the time limits specified in MCR 7.210, the full transcript of all proceedings, and provide for the payment of the reporter's fees.

(g) The trial court must serve MAACS with a copy of its order granting or denying a request for a lawyer. Unless MAACS has agreed to provide the order to any of the following, the trial court must also serve a copy of its order on the defendant, defense counsel, the prosecutor, and, if the order includes transcripts, the court reporter(s)/recorder(s). If the order is in the form of a Claim of Appeal and Appointment of Counsel, the court must also serve the Court of Appeals with a copy of the order and the judgment being appealed.

(2) Scope of Appellate Lawyer's Responsibilities. The responsibilities of the appellate lawyer appointed to represent the defendant include representing the defendant

(a) in available postconviction proceedings in the trial court the lawyer deems appropriate,

(b) in postconviction proceedings in the Court of Appeals,

(c) in available proceedings in the trial court the lawyer deems appropriate under MCR 7.208(B) or 7.211(C)(1), and

(d) as appellee in relation to any postconviction appeal taken by the prosecutor.

RULE 6.427 JUDGMENT

Within 7 days after sentencing, the court must date and sign a written judgment of sentence that includes:

(1) the title and file number of the case;

(2) the defendant's name;

(3) the crime for which the defendant was convicted;

(4) the defendant's plea;

(5) the name of the defendant's attorney if one appeared;

(6) the jury's verdict or the finding of guilt by the court;

(7) the term of the sentence;

(8) the place of detention;

(9) the conditions incident to the sentence;

(10) whether the conviction is reportable to the Secretary of State pursuant to statute, and, if so, the defendant's Michigan driver's license number; and

(11) the dollar amount of restitution that the defendant is ordered to pay.

If the defendant was found not guilty or for any other reason is entitled to be discharged, the court must enter judgment accordingly. The date a judgment is signed is its entry date.

RULE 6.428 REISSUANCE OF JUDGMENT.

If the defendant did not appeal within the time allowed by MCR 7.204(A)(2) and demonstrates that the attorney or attorneys retained or appointed to represent the defendant on direct appeal from the judgment either disregarded the defendant's instruction to perfect a timely appeal of right, or otherwise failed to provide effective assistance, and, but for counsel's deficient performance, the defendant would have perfected a timely appeal of right, the trial court shall issue an order restarting the time in which to file an appeal of right.

RULE 6.429 CORRECTION AND APPEAL OF SENTENCE

(A) Authority to Modify Sentence. The court may correct an invalid sentence, on its own initiative after giving the parties an opportunity to be heard, or on motion by either party. But the court may not modify a valid sentence after it has been imposed except as provided by law. Any correction of an invalid sentence on the court's own initiative must occur within 6 months of the entry of the judgment of conviction and sentence.

(B) Time For Filing Motion.

(1) A motion to correct an invalid sentence may be filed before the filing of a timely claim of appeal.

(2) If a claim of appeal has been filed, a motion to correct an invalid sentence may only be filed in accordance with the procedure set forth in MCR 7.208(B) or the remand procedure set forth in MCR 7.211(C)(1).

(3) If the defendant may only appeal by leave or fails to file a timely claim of appeal, a motion to correct an invalid sentence may be filed:

(a) within 6 months of entry of the judgment of conviction and sentence, or,

(b) if 6 months have elapsed since entry of the judgment of conviction and sentence, the defendant may file a motion to correct an invalid sentence if:

(i) the defendant has filed a request for the appointment of counsel pursuant to MCR 6.425(G)(1) within the 6-month period,

(ii) The defendant or defendant's lawyer, if one is appointed, has ordered the appropriate transcripts within 28 days of service of the order granting or denying the request for counsel or substitute counsel, unless the transcript has already been filed or has been ordered by the court under MCR 6.425(G), and

(iii) The motion to correct invalid sentence is filed in accordance with the provisions of this subrule within 42 days after the filing of the transcript. If the transcript was filed before the order appointing counsel or substitute counsel, or the order or denying the appointment of counsel, the 42-day period runs from the date of that order.

(4) If the defendant is no longer entitled to appeal by right or by leave, the defendant may seek relief pursuant to the procedure set forth in subchapter 6.500.

(5) If a motion to correct an invalid sentence is received by the court after the expiration of the periods set forth above, and if the appellant is an inmate in the custody of the Michigan Department of Corrections and has submitted the motion as a pro se party, the motion shall be deemed presented for filing on the date of deposit of the motion in the outgoing mail at the correctional institution in which the inmate is housed. Timely filing may be shown by a sworn statement filed with the motion, which must set forth the date of deposit and state that first-class postage has been prepaid. The exception applies to cases in which a judgment of conviction and sentence is entered on or after the effective date of this amendment. This exception also applies to an inmate housed in a penal institution in another state or in a federal penal institution who seeks to correct an invalid sentence in a Michigan court.

(C) Preservation of Issues Concerning Sentencing Guidelines Scoring and Information Considered in Sentencing. A party shall not raise on appeal an issue challenging the scoring of the sentencing guidelines or challenging the accuracy of information relied upon in determining a sentence that is within the appropriate guidelines sentence range unless the party has raised the issue at sentencing, in a proper motion for resentencing, or in a proper motion to remand filed in the court of appeals.

RULE 6.430 POSTJUDGMENT MOTION TO AMEND RESTITUTION

(A) The court may amend an order of restitution entered under this section on a motion filed by the prosecuting attorney, the victim, or the defendant based upon new or updated information related to the injury, damages, or loss for which the restitution was ordered.

(B) Filing. The moving party must file the motion and a copy of the motion with the clerk of the court in which the defendant was convicted and sentenced. Upon receipt of a motion, the clerk shall file it under the same case number as the original conviction. If an appeal is pending when the motion is filed, the moving party must serve a copy on the appellate court.

(C) Service and Notice of Hearing. If the defendant is the moving party, he/she shall serve a copy of the motion and notice of its filing on the prosecuting attorney and the prosecutor shall then serve a copy of the motion and notice upon the victim. If the prosecutor is the moving party, he/she shall serve a copy of the motion and notice of its filing on the defendant and the victim. If the victim is the moving party, he/she shall serve a copy of the motion and notice of its filing on the defendant and the prosecutor. The home address, home telephone number, work address, and work telephone number of the victim, if included on a motion to amend restitution, is nonpublic. The non-moving party is permitted but not required to respond. Any response to the motion shall comply with the time for service of the response as provided in MCR 2.119(C)(2). The court shall provide written notice of hearing on the motion to the defendant and prosecutor. The prosecutor shall then serve notice of hearing upon the victim.

(D) Appearance. As permitted by MCR 6.006(A), the court may allow the defendant to appear by two-way interactive video technology to conduct the proceeding between a courtroom and a prison, jail, or other location.

(E) Ruling. The court, in writing, shall enter an appropriate order disposing of the motion and, if the motion is granted, enter an order amending the restitution. If an appeal was pending when the motion was filed, the moving party must provide a copy of the order to the appellate court.

(F) Appeal. An appeal from this subsection is processed as provided by MCR 7.100 *et seq.*, and 7.200 *et seq.*

RULE 6.431 NEW TRIAL

(A) Time for Making Motion.

(1) A motion for a new trial may be filed before the filing of a timely claim of appeal.

(2) If a claim of appeal has been filed, a motion for a new trial may only be filed in accordance with the procedure set forth in MCR 7.208(B) or the remand procedure set forth in MCR 7.211(C)(1).

(3) If the defendant may only appeal by leave or fails to file a timely claim of appeal, a motion for a new trial may be filed:

(a) within 6 months of entry of the judgment of conviction and sentence, or

(b) If 6 months have elapsed since entry of the judgment of conviction and sentence, the defendant may file a motion for new trial if:

(i) the defendant has filed a request for the appointment of counsel pursuant to MCR 6.425(G)(1) within the 6-month period,

(ii) the defendant or defendant's lawyer, if one is appointed, has ordered the appropriate transcripts within 28 days of service of the order granting or denying the request for counsel or substitute counsel, unless the transcript has already been filed or has been ordered by the court under MCR 6.425(G), and

(iii) the motion for a new trial is filed in accordance with the provisions of this subrule within 42 days after the filing of the transcript. If the transcript was filed before the order appointing counsel or substitute counsel, or the order denying the appointment of counsel, the 42-day period runs from the date of that order.

(4) If the defendant is no longer entitled to appeal by right or by leave, the defendant may seek relief pursuant to the procedure set forth in subchapter 6.500.

(5) If a motion for new trial is received by the court after the expiration of the periods set forth above, and if the appellant is an inmate in the custody of the Michigan Department of Corrections and has submitted the motion as a pro se party, the motion shall be deemed presented for filing on the date of deposit of the motion in the outgoing mail at the correctional institution in which the inmate is housed. Timely filing may be shown by a sworn statement filed with the motion, which must set forth the date of deposit and state that first-class postage has been prepaid. The exception applies to cases in which the trial court rendered its decision on or after the effective date of this amendment. This exception also applies to an inmate housed in a penal institution in another state or in a federal penal institution who seeks a new trial in a Michigan court.

(B) Reasons for Granting. On the defendant's motion, the court may order a new trial on any ground that would support appellate reversal of the conviction or because it believes that the verdict has resulted in a miscarriage of justice. The court must state its reasons for granting or denying a new trial orally on the record or in a written ruling made a part of the record.

(C) Trial Without Jury. If the court tried the case without a jury, it may, on granting a new trial and with the defendant's consent, vacate any judgment it has entered, take additional testimony, amend its findings of fact and conclusions of law, and order the entry of a new judgment.

(D) Inclusion of Motion for Judgment of Acquittal. The court must consider a motion for a new trial challenging the weight or sufficiency of the evidence as including a motion for a directed verdict of acquittal.

RULE 6.433 DOCUMENTS FOR POSTCONVICTION PROCEEDINGS; INDIGENT DEFENDANT

(A) Appeals of Right. An indigent defendant may file a written request with the sentencing court for specified court documents or transcripts, indicating that they are required to pursue an appeal of right. The court must order the clerk to provide the defendant with copies of documents without cost to the defendant, and, unless the transcript has already been ordered as provided in MCR 6.425(G), must order the preparation of the transcript.

(B) Appeals by Leave. An indigent defendant who may file an application for leave to appeal may obtain copies of transcripts and other documents as provided in this subrule.

(1) The defendant must make a written request to the sentencing court for specified documents or transcripts indicating that they are required to prepare an application for leave to appeal.

(2) If the requested materials have been filed with the court and not provided previously to the defendant, the court clerk must provide a copy to the defendant. If the requested materials have been provided previously to the defendant, on defendant's showing of good cause to the court, the clerk must provide the defendant with another copy.

(3) If the request includes the transcript of a proceeding that has not been transcribed, the court must order the materials transcribed and filed with court. After the transcript has been prepared, court clerk must provide a copy to the defendant.

(C) Other Postconviction Proceedings. An indigent defendant who is not eligible to file an appeal of right or an application for leave to appeal may obtain records and documents as provided in this subrule.

(1) The defendant must make a written request to the sentencing court for specific court documents or transcripts indicating that the materials are required to pursue postconviction remedies in a state or federal court and are not otherwise available to the defendant.

(2) If the documents or transcripts have been filed with the court and not provided previously to the defendant, the clerk must provide the defendant with copies of such materials without cost to the defendant. If the requested materials have been provided previously to the defendant, on defendant's showing of good cause to the court, the clerk must provide the defendant with another copy.

(3) The court may order the transcription of additional proceedings if it finds that there is good cause for doing so. After such a transcript has been prepared, the clerk must provide a copy to the defendant.

(4) Nothing in this rule precludes the court from ordering materials to be supplied to the defendant in a proceeding under subchapter 6.500.

RULE 6.435 CORRECTING MISTAKES

(A) Clerical Mistakes. Clerical mistakes in judgments, orders, or other parts of the record and errors arising from oversight or omission may be corrected by the court at any time on its own initiative or on motion of a party, and after notice if the court orders it.

(B) Substantive Mistakes. After giving the parties an opportunity to be heard, and provided it has not yet entered judgment in the case, the court may reconsider and modify, correct, or rescind any order it concludes was erroneous.

(C) Correction of Record. If a dispute arises as to whether the record accurately reflects what occurred in the trial court, the court, after giving the parties the opportunity to be heard, must resolve the dispute and, if necessary, order the record to be corrected.

(D) Correction During Appeal. If a claim of appeal has been filed or leave to appeal granted in the case, corrections under this rule are subject to MCR 7.208(A) and (B).

RULE 6.440 DISABILITY OF JUDGE

(A) During Jury Trial. If, by reason of death, sickness, or other disability, the judge before whom a jury trial has commenced is unable to continue with the trial, another judge regularly sitting in or assigned to the court, on certification of having become familiar with the record of the trial, may proceed with and complete the trial.

(B) During Bench Trial. If a judge becomes disabled during a trial without a jury, another judge may be substituted for the disabled judge, but only if
    (1) both parties consent in writing to the substitution, and
    (2) the judge certifies having become familiar with the record of the trial, including the testimony previously given.

(C) After Verdict. If, after a verdict is returned or findings of fact and conclusions of law are filed, the trial judge because of disability becomes unable to perform the remaining duties the court must perform, another judge regularly sitting in or assigned to the court may perform those duties; but if that judge is not satisfied of an ability to perform those duties because of not having presided at the trial or determines that it is appropriate for any other reason, the judge may grant the defendant a new trial.

RULE 6.445 PROBATION REVOCATION

(A) Issuance of Summons; Warrant. On finding probable cause to believe that a probationer has violated a condition of probation, the court may
    (1) issue a summons in accordance with MCR 6.103(B) and (C) for the probationer to appear for arraignment on the alleged violation, or
    (2) issue a warrant for the arrest of the probationer.
    An arrested probationer must promptly be brought before the court for arraignment on the alleged violation.

(B) Arraignment on the Charge. At the arraignment on the alleged probation violation, the court must
    (1) ensure that the probationer receives written notice of the alleged violation,

(2) advise the probationer that

    (a) the probationer has a right to contest the charge at a hearing, and

    (b) the probationer is entitled to a lawyer's assistance at the hearing and at all subsequent court proceedings, and that the court will appoint a lawyer at public expense if the probationer wants one and is financially unable to retain one,

(3) if requested and appropriate, appoint a lawyer,

(4) determine what form of release, if any, is appropriate, and

(5) subject to subrule (C), set a reasonably prompt hearing date or postpone the hearing.

(C) Scheduling or Postponement of Hearing. The hearing of a probationer being held in custody for an alleged probation violation must be held within 14 days after the arraignment or the court must order the probationer released from that custody pending the hearing. If the alleged violation is based on a criminal offense that is a basis for a separate criminal prosecution, the court may postpone the hearing for the outcome of that prosecution.

(D) Continuing Duty to Advise of Right to Assistance of Lawyer. Even though a probationer charged with probation violation has waived the assistance of a lawyer, at each subsequent proceeding the court must comply with the advice and waiver procedure in MCR 6.005(E).

(E) The Violation Hearing.

    (1) Conduct of the Hearing. The evidence against the probationer must be disclosed to the probationer. The probationer has the right to be present at the hearing, to present evidence, and to examine and cross-examine witnesses. The court may consider only evidence that is relevant to the violation alleged, but it need not apply the rules of evidence except those pertaining to privileges. The state has the burden of proving a violation by a preponderance of the evidence.

    (2) Judicial Findings. At the conclusion of the hearing, the court must make findings in accordance with MCR 6.403.

(F) Pleas of Guilty. The probationer may, at the arraignment or afterward, plead guilty to the violation. Before accepting a guilty plea, the court, speaking directly to the probationer and receiving the probationer's response, must

    (1) advise the probationer that by pleading guilty the probationer is giving up the right to a contested hearing and, if the probationer is proceeding without legal representation, the right to a lawyer's assistance as set forth in subrule (B)(2)(b),

    (2) advise the probationer of the maximum possible jail or prison sentence for the offense,

    (3) ascertain that the plea is understandingly, voluntarily, and accurately made, and

    (4) establish factual support for a finding that the probationer is guilty of the alleged violation.

(G) Sentencing. If the court finds that the probationer has violated a condition of probation, or if the probationer pleads guilty to a violation, the court may continue probation, modify the conditions of probation, extend the probation period, or revoke probation and impose a sentence of incarceration. The court may not sentence the probationer to prison without having considered a current presentence report and may not sentence the probationer to prison or jail (including for failing to pay fines, costs, restitution, and other financial obligations imposed by the court) without having complied with the provisions set forth in MCR 6.425(B) and (E).

(H) Review.

(1) In a case involving a sentence of incarceration under subrule (G), the court must advise the probationer on the record, immediately after imposing sentence, that

(a) the probationer has a right to appeal, if the underlying conviction occurred as a result of a trial, or

(b) the probationer is entitled to file an application for leave to appeal, if the underlying conviction was the result of a plea of guilty or nolo contendere.

(2) In a case that involves a sentence other than incarceration under subrule (G), the court must advise the probationer on the record, immediately after imposing sentence, that the probationer is entitled to file an application for leave to appeal.

Subchapter 6.500 Postappeal Relief

Rule 6.501 Scope of Subchapter

Unless otherwise specified by these rules, a judgment of conviction and sentence entered by the circuit court not subject to appellate review under subchapters 7.200 or 7.300 may be reviewed only in accordance with the provisions of this subchapter.

RULE 6.502 MOTION FOR RELIEF FROM JUDGMENT

(A) Nature of Motion. The request for relief under this subchapter must be in the form of a motion to set aside or modify the judgment. The motion must specify all of the grounds for relief which are available to the defendant and of which the defendant has, or by the exercise of due diligence, should have knowledge.

(B) Limitations on Motion. A motion may seek relief from one judgment only. If the defendant desires to challenge the validity of additional judgments, the defendant must do so by separate motions. For the purpose of this rule, multiple convictions resulting from a single trial or plea proceeding shall be treated as a single judgment.

(C) Form of Motion. The motion may not be noticed for hearing, and must be typed or legibly handwritten and include a verification by the defendant or defendant's lawyer in accordance with MCR 1.109(D)(3). Except as otherwise ordered by the court, the combined length of the motion and any memorandum of law in support may not exceed 50 pages double-spaced, exclusive of attachments and exhibits. If the court enters an order increasing the page limit for the motion, the same order shall indicate that the page limit for the prosecutor's response provided for in MCR 6.506(A) is increased by the same amount. The motion must be substantially in the form approved by the State Court Administrative Office, and must include:

(1) The name of the defendant;

(2) The name of the court in which the defendant was convicted and the file number of the defendant's case;

(3) The place where the defendant is confined, or, if not confined, the defendant's current address;

(4) The offenses for which the defendant was convicted and sentenced;

(5) The date on which the defendant was sentenced;

(6) Whether the defendant was convicted by a jury, by a judge without jury, or on a plea of guilty, guilty but mentally ill, or nolo contendere;

(7) The sentence imposed (probation, fine, and/or imprisonment), the length of the sentence imposed, and whether the defendant is now serving that sentence;

(8) The name of the judge who presided at trial and imposed sentence;

(9) The court, title, and file number of any proceeding (including appeals and federal court proceedings) instituted by the defendant to obtain relief from conviction or sentence, specifying whether a proceeding is pending or has been completed;

(10) The name of each lawyer who represented the defendant at any time after arrest, and the stage of the case at which each represented the defendant;

(11) The relief requested;

(12) The grounds for the relief requested;

(13) The facts supporting each ground, stated in summary form;

(14) Whether any of the grounds for the relief requested were raised before; if so, at what stage of the case, and, if not, the reasons they were not raised;

(15) Whether the defendant requests the appointment of counsel, and, if so, information necessary for the court to determine whether the defendant is entitled to appointment of counsel at public expense.

Upon request, the clerk of each court with trial level jurisdiction over felony cases shall make available blank motion forms without charge to any person desiring to file such a motion.

(D) Return of Insufficient Motion. If a motion is not submitted on a form approved by the State Court Administrative Office, or does not substantially comply with the requirements of these rules, the court shall either direct that it be returned to the defendant with a statement of the reasons for its return, along with the appropriate form, or adjudicate the motion under the provisions of these rules. The clerk of the court shall retain a copy of the motion.

(E) Attachments to Motion. The defendant may attach to the motion any affidavit, document, or evidence to support the relief requested.

(F) Amendment and Supplementation of Motion. The court may permit the defendant to amend or supplement the motion at any time.

(G) Successive Motions.

(1) Except as provided in subrule (G)(2), regardless of whether a defendant has previously filed a motion for relief from judgment, after August 1, 1995, one and only one motion for relief from judgment may be filed with regard to a conviction. The court shall return without filing any successive motions for relief from judgment. A defendant may not appeal the denial or rejection of a successive motion.

(2) A defendant may file a second or subsequent motion based on a retroactive change in law that occurred after the first motion for relief from judgment or a claim of new evidence that was not discovered before the first such motion. The clerk shall refer a successive motion that asserts that one of these exceptions is applicable to the judge to whom the case is assigned for a determination whether the motion is within one of the exceptions.

The court may waive the provisions of this rule if it concludes that there is a significant possibility that the defendant is innocent of the crime.

(3) For purposes of subrule (G)(2), "new evidence" includes new scientific evidence. This includes, but is not limited to, shifts in science entailing changes:

(a) in a field of scientific knowledge, including shifts in scientific consensus;

(b) in a testifying expert's own scientific knowledge and opinions; or

(c) in a scientific method on which the relevant scientific evidence at trial was based.

RULE 6.503 FILING AND SERVICE OF MOTION

(A) Filing; Copies.

(1) A defendant seeking relief under this subchapter must file a motion, and a copy of the motion with the clerk of the court in which the defendant was convicted and sentenced.

(2) Upon receipt of a motion, the clerk shall file it under the same number as the original conviction.

(B) Service. The defendant shall serve a copy of the motion and notice of its filing on the prosecuting attorney. Unless so ordered by the court as provided in this subchapter, the filing and service of the motion does not require a response by the prosecutor.

RULE 6.504 ASSIGNMENT; PRELIMINARY CONSIDERATION BY JUDGE; SUMMARY DENIAL

(A) Assignment to Judge. The motion shall be presented to the judge to whom the case was assigned at the time of the defendant's conviction. If the appropriate judge is not available, the motion must be assigned to another judge in accordance with the court's procedure for the reassignment of cases. The chief judge may reassign cases in order to correct docket control problems arising from the requirements of this rule.

(B) Initial Consideration by Court.

(1) The court shall promptly examine the motion, together with all the files, records, transcripts, and correspondence relating to the judgment under attack. The court may request that the prosecutor provide copies of transcripts, briefs, or other records.

(2) If it plainly appears from the face of the materials described in subrule (B)(1) that the defendant is not entitled to relief, the court shall deny the motion without directing further proceedings. The order must include a concise statement of the reasons for the denial. The clerk shall serve a copy of the order on the defendant and the prosecutor. The court may dismiss some requests for relief or grounds for relief while directing a response or further proceedings with respect to other specified grounds.

(3) If the motion is summarily dismissed under subrule (B)(2), the defendant may move for reconsideration of the dismissal within 21 days after the clerk serves the order. The motion must concisely state why the court's decision was based on a clear error and that a different decision must result from correction of the error. A motion which merely presents the same matters that were considered by the court will not be granted.

(4) If the entire motion is not dismissed under subrule (B)(2), the court shall order the prosecuting attorney to file a response as provided in MCR 6.506, and shall conduct further proceedings as provided in MCR 6.505-6.508.

RULE 6.505 RIGHT TO LEGAL ASSISTANCE

(A) Appointment of Counsel. If the defendant has requested appointment of counsel, and the court has determined that the defendant is indigent, the court may appoint counsel for the defendant at any time during the proceedings under this subchapter. Counsel must be appointed if the court directs that oral argument or an evidentiary hearing be held.

(B) Opportunity to Supplement the Motion. If the court appoints counsel to represent the defendant, it shall afford counsel 56 days to amend or supplement the motion. The court may extend the time on a showing that a necessary transcript or record is not available to counsel.

RULE 6.506 RESPONSE BY PROSECUTOR

(A) Contents of Response. On direction of the court pursuant to MCR 6.504(B)(4), the prosecutor shall respond in writing to the allegations in the motion. The trial court shall allow the prosecutor a minimum of 56 days to respond. If the response refers to transcripts or briefs that are not in the court's file, the prosecutor shall submit copies of those items with the response. Except as otherwise ordered by the court, the response shall not exceed 50 pages double-spaced, exclusive of attachments and exhibits.

(B) Filing and Service. The prosecutor shall file the response and one copy with the clerk of the court and serve one copy on the defendant.

RULE 6.507 EXPANSION OF RECORD

(A) Order to Expand Record. If the court does not deny the motion pursuant to MCR 6.504(B)(2), it may direct the parties to expand the record by including any additional materials it deems relevant to the decision on the merits of the motion. The expanded record may include letters, affidavits, documents, exhibits, and answers under oath to interrogatories propounded by the court.

(B) Submission to Opposing Party. Whenever a party submits items to expand the record, the party shall serve copies of the items to the opposing party. The court shall afford the opposing party an opportunity to admit or deny the correctness of the items.

(C) Authentication. The court may require the authentication of any item submitted under this rule.

RULE 6.508 PROCEDURE; EVIDENTIARY HEARING; DETERMINATION

(A) Procedure Generally. If the rules in this subchapter do not prescribe the applicable procedure, the court may proceed in any lawful manner. The court may apply the rules applicable to civil or criminal proceedings, as it deems appropriate.

(B) Decision Without Evidentiary Hearing. After reviewing the motion and response, the record, and the expanded record, if any, the court shall determine whether an evidentiary hearing is required. If the court decides that an evidentiary hearing is not required, it may rule on the motion or, in its discretion, afford the parties an opportunity for oral argument.

(C) Evidentiary Hearing. If the court decides that an evidentiary hearing is required, it shall schedule and conduct the hearing as promptly as practicable. At the hearing, the rules of evidence other than those with respect to privilege do not apply. The court shall assure that a verbatim record is made of the hearing.

(D) Entitlement to Relief. The defendant has the burden of establishing entitlement to the relief requested. The court may not grant relief to the defendant if the motion

(1) seeks relief from a judgment of conviction and sentence that still is subject to challenge on appeal pursuant to subchapter 7.200 or subchapter 7.300;

(2) alleges grounds for relief which were decided against the defendant in a prior appeal or proceeding under this subchapter, unless the defendant establishes that a retroactive change in the law has undermined the prior decision; for purposes of this

provision, a court is not precluded from considering previously decided claims in the context of a new claim for relief, such as in determining whether new evidence would make a different result probable on retrial, or if the previously decided claims, when considered together with the new claim for relief, create a significant possibility of actual innocence;

(3) alleges grounds for relief, other than jurisdictional defects, which could have been raised on appeal from the conviction and sentence or in a prior motion under this subchapter, unless the defendant demonstrates

(a) good cause for failure to raise such grounds on appeal or in the prior motion, and

(b) actual prejudice from the alleged irregularities that support the claim for relief. As used in this subrule, "actual prejudice" means that,

(i) in a conviction following a trial,

(A) but for the alleged error, the defendant would have had a reasonably likely chance of acquittal; or

(B) where the defendant rejected a plea based on incorrect information from the trial court or ineffective assistance of counsel, it is reasonably likely that

(1) the prosecutor would not have withdrawn any plea offer;

(2) the defendant and the trial court would have accepted the plea but for the improper advice; and

(3) the conviction or sentence, or both, under the plea's terms would have been less severe than under the judgment and sentence that in fact were imposed.

(ii) in a conviction entered on a plea of guilty, guilty but mentally ill, or nolo contendere, the defect in the proceedings was such that it renders the plea an involuntary one to a degree that it would be manifestly unjust to allow the conviction to stand;

(iii) in any case, the irregularity was so offensive to the maintenance of a sound judicial process that the conviction should not be allowed to stand regardless of its effect on the outcome of the case;

(iv) in the case of a challenge to the sentence, the sentence is invalid.

The court may waive the "good cause" requirement of subrule (D)(3)(a) if it concludes that there is a significant possibility that the defendant is innocent of the crime.

(E) Ruling. The court, either orally or in writing, shall set forth in the record its findings of fact and its conclusions of law, and enter an appropriate order disposing of the motion.

RULE 6.509 APPEAL

(A) Availability of Appeal. Appeals from decisions under this subchapter are by application for leave to appeal to the Court of Appeals pursuant to MCR 7.205. The 6-month time limit provided by MCR 7.205(G)(3), runs from the decision under this subchapter. Nothing in this subchapter shall be construed as extending the time to appeal from the original judgment.

(B) Responsibility of Appointed Counsel. If the trial court has appointed counsel for the defendant during the proceeding, that appointment authorizes the attorney to represent the defendant in connection with an application for leave to appeal to the Court of Appeals.

(C) Responsibility of the Prosecutor. If the prosecutor has not filed a response to the defendant's application for leave to appeal in the appellate court, the prosecutor must file an appellee's brief if the appellate court grants the defendant's application for leave to appeal. The prosecutor must file an appellee's brief within 56 days after an order directing a response pursuant to subrule (D).

(D) Responsibility of the Appellate Court. If the appellate court grants the defendant's application for leave to appeal and the prosecutor has not filed a response in the appellate court, the appellate court must direct the prosecutor to file an appellee's brief, and give the prosecutor the opportunity to file an appellee's brief pursuant to subrule (C), before granting further relief to the defendant.

Subchapter 6.600 Criminal Procedure in District Court

Rule 6.610 Criminal Procedure Generally

(A) Precedence. Criminal cases have precedence over civil actions.

(B) Pretrial. The court, on its own initiative or on motion of either party, may direct the prosecutor and the defendant, and, if represented, the defendant's attorney to appear for a pretrial conference. The court may require collateral matters and pretrial motions to be filed and argued no later than this conference.

(C) Record. Unless a writing is permitted, a verbatim record of the proceedings before a court under subrules (D)-(F) must be made.

(D) Arraignment; District Court Offenses.

(1) Whenever a defendant is arraigned on an offense over which the district court has jurisdiction, the defendant must be informed of

(a) the name of the offense;

(b) the maximum sentence permitted by law; and

(c) the defendant's right

(i) to the assistance of an attorney and to a trial;

(ii) (if subrule [D][2] applies) to an appointed attorney; and

(iii) to a trial by jury, when required by law.

The information may be given in a writing that is made a part of the file or by the court on the record.

(2) An indigent defendant has a right to an appointed attorney whenever the offense charged requires on conviction a minimum term in jail or the court determines it might sentence to a term of incarceration, even if suspended.

If an indigent defendant is without an attorney and has not waived the right to an appointed attorney, the court may not sentence the defendant to jail or to a suspended jail sentence.

(3) The right to the assistance of an attorney, to an appointed attorney, or to a trial by jury is not waived unless the defendant

(a) has been informed of the right; and

(b) has waived it in a writing that is made a part of the file or orally on the record.

(4) The court may allow a defendant to enter a plea of not guilty or to stand mute without formal arraignment by filing a written statement signed by the defendant and any defense attorney of record, reciting the general nature of the charge, the maximum possible sentence, the rights of the defendant at arraignment, and the plea to be entered. The court may require that an appropriate bond be executed and filed

and appropriate and reasonable sureties posted or continued as a condition precedent to allowing the defendant to be arraigned without personally appearing before the court.

(E) Discovery in Misdemeanor Proceedings.

(1) The provisions of MCR 6.201, except for MCR 6.201(A), apply in all misdemeanor proceedings.

(2) MCR 6.201(A) only applies in misdemeanor proceedings, as set forth in this subrule, if a defendant elects to request discovery pursuant to MCR 6.201(A). If a defendant requests discovery pursuant to MCR 6.201(A) and the prosecuting attorney complies, then the defendant must also comply with MCR 6.201(A).

(F) Pleas of Guilty and Nolo Contendere. Before accepting a plea of guilty or nolo contendere, the court shall in all cases comply with this rule.

(1) The court shall determine that the plea is understanding, voluntary, and accurate. In determining the accuracy of the plea,

(a) if the defendant pleads guilty, the court, by questioning the defendant, shall establish support for a finding that defendant is guilty of the offense charged or the offense to which the defendant is pleading, or

(b) if the defendant pleads nolo contendere, the court shall not question the defendant about the defendant's participation in the crime, but shall make the determination on the basis of other available information.

(2) The court shall inform the defendant of the right to the assistance of an attorney. If the offense charged requires on conviction a minimum term in jail, the court shall inform the defendant that if the defendant is indigent the defendant has the right to an appointed attorney. The court shall also give such advice if it determines that it might sentence to a term of incarceration, even if suspended.

(3) The court shall advise the defendant of the following:

(a) the mandatory minimum jail sentence, if any, and the maximum possible penalty for the offense,

(b) that if the plea is accepted the defendant will not have a trial of any kind and that the defendant gives up the following rights that the defendant would have at trial:

(i) the right to have witnesses called for the defendant's defense at trial,

(ii) the right to cross-examine all witnesses called against the defendant,

(iii) the right to testify or to remain silent without an inference being drawn from said silence,

(iv) the presumption of innocence and the requirement that the defendant's guilt be proven beyond a reasonable doubt.

(4) A defendant or defendants may be informed of the trial rights listed in subrule (3)(b) as follows:

(a) on the record,

(b) in a writing made part of the file, or

(c) in a writing referred to on the record.

Except as provided in subrule (E)(7), if the court uses a writing pursuant to subrule (E)(4)(b) or (c), the court shall address the defendant and obtain from the defendant orally on the record a statement that the rights were read and understood and a waiver of those rights. The waiver may be obtained without repeating the individual rights.

(5) The court shall make the plea agreement a part of the record and determine that the parties agree on all the terms of that agreement. The court shall accept, reject or indicate on what basis it accepts the plea.

(6) The court must ask the defendant:

(a) (if there is no plea agreement) whether anyone has promised the defendant anything, or (if there is a plea agreement) whether anyone has promised anything beyond what is in the plea agreement;

(b) whether anyone has threatened the defendant; and

(c) whether it is the defendant's own choice to plead guilty.

(7) A plea of guilty or nolo contendere in writing is permissible without a personal appearance of the defendant and without support for a finding that defendant is guilty of the offense charged or the offense to which the defendant is pleading if

(a) the court decides that the combination of the circumstances and the range of possible sentences makes the situation proper for a plea of guilty or nolo contendere;

(b) the defendant acknowledges guilt or nolo contendere, in a writing to be placed in the district court file, and waives in writing the rights enumerated in subrule (3)(b); and

(c) the court is satisfied that the waiver is voluntary.

A "writing" includes digital communications, transmitted through electronic means, which are capable of being stored and printed.

(8) The following provisions apply where a defendant seeks to challenge the plea.

(a) A defendant may not challenge a plea on appeal unless the defendant moved in the trial court to withdraw the plea for noncompliance with these rules. Such a motion may be made either before or after sentence has been imposed. After imposition of sentence, the defendant may file a motion to withdraw the plea within the time for filing an application for leave to appeal under MCR 7.105(G)(2).

(b) If the trial court determines that a deviation affecting substantial rights occurred, it shall correct the deviation and give the defendant the option of permitting the plea to stand or of withdrawing the plea. If the trial court determines either a deviation did not occur, or that the deviation did not affect substantial rights, it may permit the defendant to withdraw the plea only if it does not cause substantial prejudice to the people because of reliance on the plea.

(c) If a deviation is corrected, any appeal will be on the whole record including the subsequent advice and inquiries.

(9) The State Court Administrator shall develop and approve forms to be used under subrules (E)(4)(b) and (c) and (E)(7)(b).

(G) Sentencing.

(1) For sentencing, the court shall:

(a) require the presence of the defendant's attorney, unless the defendant does not have one or has waived the attorney's presence;

(b) provide copies of the presentence report (if a presentence report was prepared) to the prosecutor and the defendant's lawyer, or the defendant if not represented by a lawyer, at a reasonable time, but not less than two business days before the day of sentencing. The prosecutor and the defendant's lawyer, or the defendant if not represented by a lawyer, may retain a copy of the report or an amended report. If the presentence report is not made available to the prosecutor and the defendant's lawyer, or the defendant if not represented by a lawyer, at least two business days before the day of sentencing, the prosecutor and the defendant's lawyer, or the defendant if not represented by a lawyer, shall be entitled, on oral motion, to an adjournment to enable the moving party to review the presentence report and to prepare any necessary corrections, additions or deletions to present to the court, or otherwise advise the court of circumstances the prosecutor or defendant believes should be considered in imposing sentence. A presentence investigation report shall not include any address or telephone number for the home, workplace, school, or place of worship of any victim or witness, or a family member of any victim or witness, unless an address is used to identify the place of the crime or to impose conditions of release from custody that are necessary for the protection of a named individual. Upon request, any other address or telephone number that would reveal the location of a victim or witness or a family member of a victim or witness shall be exempted from disclosure unless an address is used to identify the place of the crime or to impose conditions of release from custody that are necessary for the protection of a named individual.

(c) inform the defendant of credit to be given for time served, if any.

(d) order the dollar amount of restitution that the defendant must pay to make full restitution as required by law to any victim of the defendant's course of conduct that gives rise to the conviction, or to that victim's estate. Any dispute as to the proper amount or type of restitution shall be resolved by the court by a preponderance of the evidence. The burden of demonstrating the amount of the loss sustained by a victim as a result of the offense shall be on the prosecuting attorney.

(2) The court shall not sentence a defendant to a term of incarceration for nonpayment unless the court has complied with the provisions of MCR 6.425(E)(3).

(3) Unless a defendant who is entitled to appointed counsel is represented by an attorney or has waived the right to an attorney, a subsequent charge or sentence may not be enhanced because of this conviction and the defendant may not be incarcerated for violating probation or any other condition imposed in connection with this conviction.

(4) Immediately after imposing a sentence of incarceration, even if suspended, the court must advise the defendant, on the record or in writing, that:

(a) if the defendant wishes to file an appeal and is financially unable to retain a lawyer, the court will appoint a lawyer to represent the defendant on appeal, and

(b) the request for a lawyer must be made within 14 days after sentencing.

(H) Motion for New Trial. A motion for a new trial must be filed within 21 days after the entry of judgment. However, if an appeal has not been taken, a delayed motion may be filed within the time for filing an application for leave to appeal.

(I) Arraignment; Offenses Not Cognizable by the District Court. In a prosecution in which a defendant is charged with a felony or a misdemeanor not cognizable by the district court, the court shall

(1) inform the defendant of the nature of the charge;

(2) inform the defendant of

(a) the right to a preliminary examination;

(b) the right to an attorney, if the defendant is not represented by an attorney at the arraignment;

(c) the right to have an attorney appointed at public expense if the defendant is indigent; and

(d) the right to consideration of pretrial release.

If a defendant not represented by an attorney waives the preliminary examination, the court shall ascertain that the waiver is freely, understandingly, and voluntarily given before accepting it.

RULE 6.615 MISDEMEANOR TRAFFIC CASES

(A) Citation; Complaint; Summons; Warrant.

    (1) A misdemeanor traffic case may be initiated by one of the following procedures:

        (a) Service by a law enforcement officer on the defendant of a written citation, and the filing of the citation in the district court. The citation may be prepared electronically or on paper. The citation must be signed by the officer in accordance with MCR 1.109(E)(4); if a citation is prepared electronically and filed with a court as data, the name of the officer that is associated with issuance of the citation satisfies this requirement.

        (b) The filing of a sworn complaint in the district court and the issuance of an arrest warrant. A citation may serve as the sworn complaint and as the basis for a misdemeanor warrant.

        (c) Other special procedures authorized by statute.

    (2) The citation serves as a summons to command

        (a) the initial appearance of the defendant; and

        (b) a response from the defendant as to his or her guilt of the violation alleged.

(B) Appearances; Failure To Appear. If a defendant fails to appear or otherwise to respond to any matter pending relative to a misdemeanor traffic citation, the court shall proceed as provided in this subrule.

    (1) If the defendant is a Michigan resident, the court

        (a) must initiate the procedures required by MCL 257.321a for the failure to answer a citation; and

        (b) may issue a warrant for the defendant's arrest.

    (2) If the defendant is not a Michigan resident,

        (a) the court may mail a notice to appear to the defendant at the address in the citation;

        (b) the court may issue a warrant for the defendant's arrest; and

        (c) if the court has received the driver's license of a nonresident, pursuant to statute, it may retain the license as allowed by statute. The court need not retain the license past its expiration date.

(C) Arraignment. An arraignment in a misdemeanor traffic case may be conducted by

    (1) a judge of the district, or

    (2) a district court magistrate as authorized by statute and by the judges of the district.

(D) Contested Cases. A misdemeanor traffic case must be conducted in compliance with the constitutional and statutory procedures and safeguards applicable to misdemeanors cognizable by the district court.

RULE 6.620 IMPANELING THE JURY

(A) Alternate Jurors. The court may direct that 7 or more jurors be impaneled to sit in a criminal case. After the instructions to the jury have been given and the case submitted, the names of the jurors must be placed in a container and names drawn to reduce the number of jurors to 6, who shall constitute the jury. The court may retain the alternate jurors during deliberations. If the court does so, it shall instruct the alternate jurors not to discuss the case with any other person until the jury completes its deliberations and is discharged. If an alternate juror replaces a juror after the jury retires to consider its verdict, the court shall instruct the jury to begin its deliberations anew.

(B) Peremptory Challenges.

(1) Each defendant is entitled to three peremptory challenges. The prosecutor is entitled to the same number of peremptory challenges as a defendant being tried alone, or, in the case of jointly tried defendants, the total number of peremptory challenges to which all the defendants are entitled.

(2) Additional Challenges. On a showing of good cause, the court may grant one or more of the parties an increased number of peremptory challenges. The additional challenges granted by the court need not be equal for each party.

RULE 6.625 APPEAL; APPOINTMENT OF APPELLATE COUNSEL

(A) An appeal from a misdemeanor case is governed by subchapter 7.100.

(B) If the court imposed a sentence of incarceration, even if suspended, and the defendant is indigent, the court must enter an order appointing a lawyer if, within 14 days after sentencing, the defendant files a request for a lawyer or makes a request on the record. Unless there is a postjudgment motion pending, the court must rule on a defendant's request for a lawyer within 14 days after receiving it. If there is a postjudgment motion pending, the court must rule on the request after the court's disposition of the pending motion and within 14 days after that disposition. If a lawyer is appointed, the 21 days for taking an appeal pursuant to MCR 7.104(A)(3) and MCR 7.105(A)(3) shall commence on the day of the appointment.

Subchapter 6.900 Rules Applicable to Juveniles Charged With Specified Offenses Subject to the Jurisdiction of the Circuit or District Court

Rule 6.901 Applicability

(A) Precedence. The rules in this subchapter take precedence over, but are not exclusive of, the rules of procedure applicable to criminal actions against adult offenders.

(B) Scope. The rules apply to criminal proceedings in the district court and the circuit court concerning a juvenile against whom the prosecuting attorney has authorized the filing of a criminal complaint charging a specified juvenile violation instead of approving the filing of a petition in the family division of the circuit court. The rules do not apply to a person charged solely with an offense in which the family division has waived jurisdiction pursuant to MCL712A.4.

(C) Video and Audio Proceedings. The courts may use telephonic, voice, or videoconferencing technology under this subchapter as prescribed by MCR 6.006.

Rule 6.903 Definitions

When used in this subchapter, unless the context otherwise indicates:

(A) "Commitment review hearing" includes a hearing as required by MCL 769.1 to decide whether the jurisdiction of the court shall continue over a juvenile who was placed on juvenile probation and committed to state wardship.

(B) "Commitment review report" means a report on a juvenile committed to state wardship for use at a commitment review hearing prepared by the Family Independence Agency pursuant to MCL 803.225 (§ 5 of the Juvenile Facilities Act).

(C) "Court" means the circuit court as provided in MCL 600.606, but does not include the family division of the circuit court.

(D) "Family division" means the family division of the circuit court.

(E) "Juvenile" means a person 14 years of age or older, who is subject to the jurisdiction of the court for having allegedly committed a specified juvenile violation on or after the person's 14th birthday and before the person's 17th birthday.

(F) "Juvenile sentencing hearing" means a hearing conducted by the court following a criminal conviction to determine whether the best interests of the juvenile and of the public would be served:

    (1) by retaining jurisdiction over the juvenile, placing the juvenile on juvenile probation, and committing the juvenile to a state institution or agency as a state ward, as provided in MCL 769.1; or

    (2) by imposing sentence as provided by law for an adult offender.

(G) "Juvenile facility" means an institution or facility operated by the juvenile division of the circuit court, or a state institution or agency described in the Youth Rehabilitation Services Act, MCL 803.301 *et seq.,* or a county facility or institution operated as an agency of the county other than a facility designed or used to incarcerate adults.

(H) "Specified Juvenile Violation" means one or more of the following offenses allegedly committed by a juvenile in which the prosecuting attorney has authorized the filing of a criminal complaint and warrant instead of proceeding in the family division of the circuit court:

    (1) burning a dwelling house, MCL 750.72;

    (2) assault with intent to commit murder, MCL 750.83;

    (3) assault with intent to maim, MCL 750.86;

    (4) assault with intent to rob while armed, MCL 750.89;

    (5) attempted murder, MCL 750.91;

    (6) first-degree murder, MCL 750.316;

    (7) second-degree murder, MCL 750.317;

    (8) kidnapping, MCL 750.349;

    (9) first-degree criminal sexual conduct, MCL 750.520b;

    (10) armed robbery, MCL 750.529;

    (11) carjacking, MCL 750.529a;

    (12) bank, safe, or vault robbery, MCL 750.531;

    (13) assault with intent to do great bodily harm, MCL 750.84, if armed with a dangerous weapon;

    (14) first-degree home invasion, MCL 750.110a(2), if armed with a dangerous weapon;

(15) escape or attempted escape from a medium-security or high-security juvenile facility operated by the Family Independence Agency, or a high-security facility operated by a private agency under contract with the Family Independence Agency, MCL 750.186a;

(16) possession of [MCL 333.7403(2)(a)(i)] or manufacture, delivery, or possession with intent to manufacture or deliver of 650 grams(1,000 grams beginning March 1, 2003) or more of a schedule 1 or 2 controlled substance [MCL 333.7401(2)(a)(i)];

(17) any attempt, MCL 750.92; solicitation, MCL 750.157b; or conspiracy, MCL 750.157a; to commit any of the offenses listed in subrules (1)-(16);

(18) any lesser-included offense of an offense listed in subrules (1)-(17) if the juvenile is charged with a specified juvenile violation;

(19) any other violation arising out of the same transaction if the juvenile is charged with one of the offenses listed in subrules (1)-(17).

(I) "Dangerous Weapon" means one of the following:

(1) a loaded or unloaded firearm, whether operable or inoperable;

(2) a knife, stabbing instrument, brass knuckles, blackjack, club, or other object specifically designed or customarily carried or possessed for use as a weapon;

(3) an object that is likely to cause death or bodily injury when used as a weapon and that is used as a weapon, or carried or possessed for use as a weapon;

(4) an object or device that is used or fashioned in a manner leading a person to believe the object or device is an object or device described in subrules (1)-(3).

(J) "Magistrate" means a judge of the district court or a municipal court as defined in MCL 761.1(f).

(K) "Progress report" means the report on a juvenile in state wardship prepared by the Family Independence Agency for the court as required by MCL 803.223 (§ 3 of the Juvenile Facilities Act) and by these rules.

(L) "Social report" means the written report on a juvenile for use at the juvenile sentencing hearing prepared by the Family Independence Agency as required by MCL 803.224 (§ 4 of the Juvenile Facilities Act).

(M) "State wardship" means care and control of a juvenile until the juvenile's 21st birthday by an institution or agency within or under the supervision of the Family Independence Agency as provided in the Youth Rehabilitation Services Act, MCL 803.301 *et seq.*, while the juvenile remains under the jurisdiction of the court on the basis of a court order of juvenile probation and commitment as provided in MCL 769.1.

RULE 6.905 ASSISTANCE OF ATTORNEY

(A) Advice of Right. If the juvenile is not represented by an attorney, the magistrate or court shall advise the juvenile at each stage of the criminal proceedings of the right to the assistance of an attorney. If the juvenile has waived the right to an attorney, the court at later proceedings must reaffirm that the juvenile continues to not want an attorney.

(B) Court-Appointed Attorney. Unless the juvenile has a retained attorney, or has waived the right to an attorney, the magistrate or the court must appoint an attorney to represent the juvenile.

(C) Waiver of Attorney. The magistrate or court may permit a juvenile to waive representation by an attorney if:

(1) an attorney is appointed to give the juvenile advice on the question of waiver;

(2) the magistrate or the court finds that the juvenile is literate and is competent to conduct a defense;

(3) the magistrate or the court advises the juvenile of the dangers and of the disadvantages of self-representation;

(4) the magistrate or the court finds on the record that the waiver is voluntarily and understandingly made; and

(5) the court appoints standby counsel to assist the juvenile at trial and at the juvenile sentencing hearing.

(D) Cost. The court may assess cost of legal representation, or part thereof, against the juvenile or against a person responsible for the support of the juvenile, or both. The order assessing cost shall not be binding on a person responsible for the support of the juvenile unless an opportunity for a hearing has been given and until a copy of the order is served on the person, personally or by first class mail to the person's last known address.

RULE 6.907 ARRAIGNMENT ON COMPLAINT AND WARRANT

(A) Time. When the prosecuting attorney authorizes the filing of a complaint and warrant charging a juvenile with a specified juvenile violation instead of approving the filing of a petition in the family division of the circuit court, the juvenile in custody must be taken to the magistrate for arraignment on the charge. The prosecuting attorney must make a good-faith effort to notify the parent of the juvenile of the arraignment. The juvenile must be released if arraignment has not commenced:

(1) within 24 hours of the arrest of the juvenile; or

(2) within 24 hours after the prosecuting attorney authorized the complaint and warrant during special adjournment pursuant to MCR 3.935(A)(3), provided the juvenile is being detained in a juvenile facility.

(B) Temporary Detention Pending Arraignment. If the prosecuting attorney has authorized the filing of a complaint and warrant charging a specified juvenile violation instead of approving the filing of a petition in the family division of the circuit court, a juvenile may, following apprehension, be detained pending arraignment:

(1) in a juvenile facility operated by the county;

(2) in a regional juvenile detention facility operated by the state; or

(3) in a facility operated by the family division of the circuit court with the consent of the family division or an order of a court as defined in MCR 6.903(C).

If no juvenile facility is reasonably available and if it is apparent that the juvenile may not otherwise be safely detained, the magistrate may, without a hearing, authorize that the juvenile be lodged pending arraignment in a facility used to incarcerate adults. The juvenile must be kept separate from adult prisoners as required by law.

(C) Procedure. At the arraignment on the complaint and warrant:

(1) The magistrate shall determine whether a parent, guardian, or an adult relative of the juvenile is present. Arraignment may be conducted without the presence of a parent, guardian, or adult relative provided the magistrate appoints an attorney to appear at arraignment with the juvenile or provided an attorney has been retained and appears with the juvenile.

(2) The magistrate shall set a date for the juvenile's preliminary examination within the next 14 days, less time given and used by the prosecuting attorney under special adjournment pursuant to MCR 3.935(A)(3), up to three days' credit. The magistrate shall inform the juvenile and the parent, guardian, or adult relative of the juvenile, if

present, of the preliminary examination date. If a parent, guardian, or an adult relative is not present at the arraignment, the court shall direct the attorney for the juvenile to advise a parent or guardian of the juvenile of the scheduled preliminary examination.

RULE 6.909 RELEASING OR DETAINING JUVENILES BEFORE TRIAL OR SENTENCING

(A) Bail; Detention.

(1) Bail. Except as provided in subrule (2) the magistrate or court must advise the juvenile of a right to bail as provided for an adult accused. The magistrate or the court may order a juvenile released to a parent or guardian on the basis of any lawful condition, including that bail be posted.

(2) Detention Without Bail. If the proof is evident or if the presumption is great that the juvenile committed the offense, the magistrate or the court may deny bail:

(a) to a juvenile charged with first-degree murder, second-degree murder, or

(b) to a juvenile charged with first-degree criminal sexual conduct, or armed robbery,

(i) who is likely to flee, or

(ii) who clearly presents a danger to others.

(B) Place of Confinement.

(1) Juvenile Facility. Except as provided in subrule (B)(2) and in MCR 6.907(B), a juvenile charged with a crime and not released must be placed in a juvenile facility while awaiting trial and, if necessary, sentencing, rather than being placed in a jail or similar facility designed and used to incarcerate adult prisoners.

(2) Jailing of Juveniles; Restricted. On motion of a prosecuting attorney or a superintendent of a juvenile facility in which the juvenile is detained, the magistrate or court may order the juvenile confined in a jail or similar facility designed and used to incarcerate adult prisoners upon a showing that

(a) the juvenile's habits or conduct are considered a menace to other juveniles; or

(b) the juvenile may not otherwise be safely detained in a juvenile facility.

(3) Family Division Operated Facility. The juvenile shall not be placed in an institution operated by the family division of the circuit court except with the consent of the family division or on order of a court as defined in MCR 6.903(C).

(4) Separate Custody of Juvenile. The juvenile in custody or detention must be maintained separately from the adult prisoners or adult accused as required by MCL 764.27a.

(C) Speedy Trial. Within 7 days of the filing of a motion, the court shall release a juvenile who has remained in detention while awaiting trial for more than 91 days to answer for the specified juvenile violation unless the trial has commenced. In computing the 91-day period, the court is to exclude delays as provided in MCR 6.004(C)(1)-(6) and the time required to conduct the hearing on the motion.

RULE 6.911 PRELIMINARY EXAMINATION

(A) Waiver. The juvenile may waive a preliminary examination if the juvenile is represented by an attorney and the waiver is made and signed by the juvenile in open court. The magistrate shall find and place on the record that the waiver was freely, understandingly, and voluntarily given.

(B) Transfer to Family Division of Circuit Court. If the magistrate, following preliminary examination, finds that there is no probable cause to believe that a specified juvenile violation occurred or that there is no probable cause to believe that the juvenile committed the specified juvenile violation, but that some other offense occurred that if committed by an adult would constitute a crime, and that there is probable cause to believe that the juvenile committed that offense, the magistrate shall transfer the matter to the family division of the circuit court in the county where the offense is alleged to have been committed for further proceedings. If the court transfers the matter to the family division, a transcript of the preliminary examination shall be sent to the family division without charge upon request.

RULE 6.931 JUVENILE SENTENCING HEARING

(A) General. If the juvenile has been convicted of an offense listed in MCL 769.1(1)(a)-(*l*), the court must sentence the juvenile in the same manner as an adult. Unless a juvenile is required to be sentenced in the same manner as an adult, a judge of a court having jurisdiction over a juvenile shall conduct a juvenile sentencing hearing unless the hearing is waived as provided in subrule (B). At the conclusion of the juvenile sentencing hearing, the court shall determine whether to impose a sentence against the juvenile as though an adult offender or whether to place the juvenile on juvenile probation and commit the juvenile to state wardship pursuant to MCL 769.1b.

(B) No Juvenile Sentencing Hearing; Consent. The court need not conduct a juvenile sentencing hearing if the prosecuting attorney, the juvenile, and the attorney for the juvenile, consent that it is not in the best interest of the public to sentence the juvenile as though an adult offender. If the juvenile sentence hearing is waived, the court shall not impose a sentence as provided by law for an adult offender. The court must place the juvenile on juvenile probation and commit the juvenile to state wardship.

(C) Notice of Juvenile Sentencing Hearing Following Verdict. If a juvenile sentencing hearing is required, the prosecuting attorney, the juvenile, and the attorney for the juvenile must be advised on the record immediately following conviction of the juvenile by a guilty plea or verdict of guilty that a hearing will be conducted at sentencing, unless waived, to determine whether to sentence the juvenile as an adult or to place the juvenile on juvenile probation and commit the juvenile to state wardship as though a delinquent. The court may announce the scheduled date of the hearing. On request, the court shall notify the victim of the juvenile sentencing hearing.

(D) Review of Reports. The court must give the prosecuting attorney, the juvenile, and the attorney for the juvenile, an opportunity to review the presentence report and the social report before the juvenile sentencing hearing. The court may exempt information from the reports as provided in MCL 771.14 and 771.14a.

(E) Juvenile Sentencing Hearing Procedure.

    (1) Evidence. At the juvenile sentencing hearing all relevant and material evidence may be received by the court and relied upon to the extent of its probative value, even though such evidence may not be admissible at trial. The rules of evidence do not apply. The court shall receive and consider the presentence report prepared by the probation officer and the social report prepared by the Family Independence Agency.

    (2) Standard of Proof. The court must sentence the juvenile in the same manner as an adult unless the court determines by a preponderance of the evidence, except as

provided in subrule (3)(c), that the best interests of the public would be served by placing the juvenile on probation and committing the juvenile to state wardship.

(3) Alternative Sentences For Juveniles Convicted of Certain Controlled Substance Offenses. If a juvenile is convicted of a violation or conspiracy to commit a violation of MCL 333.7403(2)(a)(i), the court shall determine whether the best interests of the public would be served by:

> (a) imposing the sentence provided by law for an adult offender;
>
> (b) placing the individual on probation and committing the individual to a state institution or agency as provided in MCL 769.1(3); or
>
> (c) imposing a sentence of imprisonment for any term of years, but not less than 25 years, if the court determines by clear and convincing evidence that such a sentence would serve the best interests of the public.

In making its determination, the court shall use the criteria set forth in subrule (4).

(4) Criteria. The court shall consider the following criteria in determining whether to sentence the juvenile as though an adult offender or whether to place the juvenile on juvenile probation and commit the juvenile to state wardship, giving more weight to the seriousness of the alleged offense and the juvenile's prior record of delinquency:

> (a) the seriousness of the alleged offense in terms of community protection, including, but not limited to, the existence of any aggravating factors recognized by the sentencing guidelines, the use of a firearm or other dangerous weapon, and the impact on any victim;
>
> (b) the culpability of the juvenile in committing the alleged offense, including, but not limited to, the level of the juvenile's participation in planning and carrying out the offense and the existence of any aggravating or mitigating factors recognized by the sentencing guidelines;
>
> (c) the juvenile's prior record of delinquency, including, but not limited to, any record of detention, any police record, any school record, or any other evidence indicating prior delinquent behavior;
>
> (d) the juvenile's programming history, including, but not limited to, the juvenile's past willingness to participate meaningfully in available programming;
>
> (e) the adequacy of the punishment or programming available in the juvenile justice system; and
>
> (f) the dispositional options available for the juvenile.

(5) Findings. The court must make findings of fact and conclusions of law forming the basis for the juvenile probation and commitment decision or the decision to sentence the juvenile as though an adult offender. The findings and conclusions may be incorporated in a written opinion or stated on the record.

(F) Postjudgment Procedure; Juvenile Probation and Commitment to State Wardship. If the court retains jurisdiction over the juvenile, places the juvenile on juvenile probation, and commits the juvenile to state wardship, the court shall comply with subrules (1)-(11):

> (1) The court shall enter a judgment that includes a provision for reimbursement by the juvenile or those responsible for the juvenile's support, or both, for the cost of care and services pursuant to MCL 769.1(7). An order assessing such cost against a person responsible for the support of the juvenile shall not be binding on the person, unless an opportunity for a hearing has been given and until a copy of the order is served on the person, personally or by first class mail to the person's last known address.

(2) The court shall advise the juvenile at sentencing that if the juvenile, while on juvenile probation, is convicted of a felony or a misdemeanor punishable by more than one year's imprisonment, the court must revoke juvenile probation and sentence the juvenile to a term of years in prison not to exceed the penalty that might have been imposed for the offense for which the juvenile was originally convicted.

(3) The court shall assure that the juvenile receives a copy of the social report.

(4) The court shall send a copy of the order and a copy of the written opinion or transcript of the findings and conclusions of law to the Family Independence Agency.

(5) The court shall not place the juvenile on deferred sentencing, as provided in MCL 771.1(2).

(6) The court shall not place the juvenile on life probation for conviction of a controlled substance violation, as set forth in MCL 771.1(4).

(7) The five-year limit on the term of probation for an adult felony offender shall not apply.

(8) The court shall not require as a condition of juvenile probation that the juvenile report to a department of corrections probation officer.

(9) The court shall not, as a condition of juvenile probation, impose jail time against the juvenile except as provided in MCR 6.933(B)(2).

(10) The court shall not commit the juvenile to the Department of Corrections for failing to comply with a restitution order.

(11) The court shall not place the juvenile in a Department of Corrections camp for one year, as otherwise provided in MCL 771.3a(1).

RULE 6.933 JUVENILE PROBATION REVOCATION

(A) General Procedure. When a juvenile, who was placed on juvenile probation and committed to an institution as a state ward, is alleged to have violated juvenile probation, the court shall proceed as provided in MCR 6.445(A)-(F).

(B) Disposition in General.

    (1) Certain Criminal Offense Violations.

        (a) If the court finds that the juvenile has violated juvenile probation by being convicted of a felony or a misdemeanor punishable by more than one year's imprisonment, the court must revoke the probation of the juvenile and order the juvenile committed to the Department of Corrections for a term of years not to exceed the penalty that could have been imposed for the offense that led to the probation. The court in imposing sentence shall grant credit against the sentence as required by law.

        (b) The court may not revoke probation and impose sentence under subrule (B)(1) unless at the original sentencing the court gave the advice, as required by MCR 6.931(F)(2), that subsequent conviction of a felony or a misdemeanor punishable by more than one year's imprisonment would result in the revocation of juvenile probation and in the imposition of a sentence of imprisonment.

    (2) Other Violations. If the court finds that the juvenile has violated juvenile probation, other than as provided in subrule (B)(1), the court may order the juvenile committed to the Department of Corrections as provided in subrule (B)(1), or may order the juvenile continued on juvenile probation and under state wardship, and may order any of the following:

        (a) a change of placement,

(b) restitution,

(c) community service,

(d) substance abuse counseling,

(e) mental health counseling,

(f) participation in a vocational-technical education program,

(g) incarceration in a county jail for not more than 30 days, and

(h) any other participation or performance as the court considers necessary.

If the court determines to place the juvenile in jail for up to 30 days, and the juvenile is under 17 years of age, the juvenile must be placed separately from adult prisoners as required by law.

(3) If the court revokes juvenile probation pursuant to subrule (B)(1), the court must receive an updated presentence report and comply with MCR 6.445(G) before it imposes a prison sentence on the juvenile.

(C) Disposition Regarding Specific Underlying Offenses.

(1) Controlled Substance Violation Punishable by Mandatory Nonparolable Life Sentence For Adults. A juvenile who was placed on probation and committed to state wardship for manufacture, delivery, or possession with the intent to deliver 650 grams(1,000 grams beginning March 1, 2003) or more of a controlled substance, MCL 333.7401(2)(a)(i), may be resentenced only to a term of years following mandatory revocation of probation for commission of a subsequent felony or a misdemeanor punishable by more than one year of imprisonment.

(2) First-Degree Murder. A juvenile convicted of first-degree murder who violates juvenile probation by being convicted of a felony or a misdemeanor punishable by more than one year's imprisonment may only be sentenced to a term of years, not to nonparolable life.

(D) Review. The juvenile may appeal as of right from the imposition of a sentence of incarceration after a finding of juvenile probation violation.

(E) Determination of Ability to Pay. A juvenile and/or parent shall not be detained or incarcerated for the nonpayment of court-ordered financial obligations as ordered by the court, unless the court determines that the juvenile and/or parent has the resources to pay and has not made a good-faith effort to do so.

RULE 6.935 PROGRESS REVIEW OF COURT-COMMITTED JUVENILES

(A) General. When a juvenile is placed on probation and committed to a state institution or agency, the court retains jurisdiction over the juvenile while the juvenile is on probation and committed to that state institution or agency. The court shall review the progress of a juvenile it has placed on juvenile probation and committed to state wardship.

(B) Time.

(1) Semiannual Progress Reviews. The court must conduct a progress review no later than 182 days after the entry of the order placing the juvenile on juvenile probation and committing the juvenile to state wardship. A review shall be made semiannually thereafter as long as the juvenile remains in state wardship.

(2) Annual Review. The court shall conduct an annual review of the services being provided to the juvenile, the juvenile's placement, and the juvenile's progress in that placement.

(C) Progress Review Report. In conducting these reviews, the court shall examine the progress review report prepared by the Family Independence Agency, covering placement and services being provided the juvenile and the progress of the juvenile, and the court shall also examine the juvenile's annual report prepared under MCL 803.223 (§ 3 of the Juvenile Facilities Act). The court may order changes in the juvenile's placement or treatment plan including, but not limited to, committing the juvenile to the jurisdiction of the Department of Corrections, on the basis of the review.

(D) Hearings for Progress and Annual Reviews. Unless the court orders a more restrictive placement or treatment plan, there shall be no requirement that the court hold a hearing when conducting a progress review for a court-committed juvenile pursuant to MCR 6.935(B). However, the court may not order a more physically restrictive change in the level of placement of the juvenile or order more restrictive treatment absent a hearing as provided in MCR 6.937.

Rule 6.937 Commitment Review Hearing

(A) Required Hearing Before Age 19 for Court-Committed Juveniles. The court shall schedule and hold, unless adjourned for good cause, a commitment review hearing as nearly as possible to, but before, the juvenile's 19th birthday.

(1) Notice. The Family Independence Agency or agency, facility, or institution to which the juvenile is committed, shall advise the court at least 91 days before the juvenile attains age 19 of the need to schedule a commitment review hearing. Notice of the hearing must be given to the prosecuting attorney, the agency or the superintendent of the facility to which the juvenile has been committed, the juvenile, and the parent of the juvenile if the parent's address or whereabouts are known, at least 14 days before the hearing. Notice must clearly indicate that the court may extend jurisdiction over the juvenile until the age of 21. The notice shall include advice to the juvenile and the parent of the juvenile that the juvenile has the right to an attorney.

(2) Appointment of an Attorney. The court must appoint an attorney to represent the juvenile at the hearing unless an attorney has been retained or is waived pursuant to MCR 6.905(C).

(3) Reports. The state institution or agency charged with the care of the juvenile must prepare a commitment report as required by MCL 769.1b(4) and 803.225(1). The commitment report must contain all of the following, as required by MCL 803.225(1)(a)-(d):

(a) the services and programs currently being utilized by, or offered to, the juvenile and the juvenile's participation in those services and programs;

(b) where the juvenile currently resides and the juvenile's behavior in the current placement;

(c) the juvenile's efforts toward rehabilitation; and

(d) recommendations for the juvenile's release or continued custody.

The report created pursuant to MCL 803.223 for the purpose of annual reviews may be combined with a commitment review report.

(4) Findings; Criteria. Before the court continues the jurisdiction over the juvenile until the age of 21, the prosecutor must demonstrate by a preponderance of the evidence that the juvenile has not been rehabilitated or that the juvenile presents a

serious risk to public safety. The rules of evidence do not apply. In making the determination, the court must consider the following factors:

    (a) the extent and nature of the juvenile's participation in education, counseling, or work programs;

    (b) the juvenile's willingness to accept responsibility for prior behavior;

    (c) the juvenile's behavior in the current placement;

    (d) the prior record and character of the juvenile and physical and mental maturity;

    (e) the juvenile's potential for violent conduct as demonstrated by prior behavior;

    (f) the recommendations of the state institution or agency charged with the juvenile's care for the juvenile's release or continued custody; and

    (g) other information the prosecuting attorney or the juvenile may submit.

(B) Other Commitment Review Hearings. The court, on motion of the institution, agency, or facility to which the juvenile is committed, may release a juvenile at any time upon a showing by a preponderance of evidence that the juvenile has been rehabilitated and is not a risk to public safety. The notice provision in subrule (A), other than the requirement that the court clearly indicate that it may extend jurisdiction over the juvenile until the age of 21, and the criteria in subrule (A) shall apply. The rules of evidence shall not apply. The court must appoint an attorney to represent the juvenile at the hearing unless an attorney has been retained or the right to counsel waived. The court, upon notice and opportunity to be heard as provided in this rule, may also move the juvenile to a more restrictive placement or treatment program.

RULE 6.938 FINAL REVIEW HEARINGS

(A) General. The court must conduct a final review of the juvenile's probation and commitment not less than 3 months before the end of the period that the juvenile is on probation and committed to the state institution or agency. If the court determines at this review that the best interests of the public would be served by imposing any other sentence provided by law for an adult offender, the court may impose that sentence.

(B) Notice Requirements. Not less than 14 days before a final review hearing is to be conducted, the prosecuting attorney, juvenile, and, if addresses are known, the juvenile's parents or guardian must be notified. The notice must state that the court may impose a sentence upon the juvenile and must advise the juvenile and the juvenile's parent or guardian of the right to legal counsel.

(C) Appointment of Counsel. If an attorney has not been retained or appointed to represent the juvenile, the court must appoint an attorney and may assess the cost of providing an attorney as costs against the juvenile or those responsible for the juvenile's support, or both, if the persons to be assessed are financially able to comply.

(D) Criteria. In determining whether the best interests of the public would be served by imposing sentence, the court shall consider the following:

    (1) the extent and nature of the juvenile's participation in education, counseling, or work programs;

    (2) the juvenile's willingness to accept responsibility for prior behavior;

    (3) the juvenile's behavior in the current placement;

    (4) the prior record and character of the juvenile and the juvenile's physical and mental maturity;

    (5) the juvenile's potential for violent conduct as demonstrated by prior behavior;

(6) the recommendations of the state institution or agency charged with the juvenile's care for the juvenile's release or continued custody;

(7) the effect of treatment on the juvenile's rehabilitation;

(8) whether the juvenile is likely to be dangerous to the public if released;

(9) the best interests of the public welfare and the protection of public security; and

(10) other information the prosecuting attorney or juvenile may submit.

(E) Credit for Time Served on Probation. If a sentence is imposed, the juvenile must receive credit for the period of time served on probation and committed to a state agency or institution.

MICHIGAN RULES OF EVIDENCE

RULES 101-106

Rule 101 Scope

These rules govern proceedings in the courts of this state to the extent and with the exceptions stated in Rule 1101. A statutory rule of evidence not in conflict with these rules or other rules adopted by the Supreme Court is effective until superseded by rule or decision of the Supreme Court.

Rule 102 Purpose

These rules are intended to secure fairness in administration, elimination of unjustifiable expense and delay, and promotion of growth and development of the law of evidence to the end that the truth may be ascertained and proceedings justly determined.

Rule 103 Rulings on Evidence

(a)   *Effect of erroneous ruling.* Error may not be predicated upon a ruling which admits or excludes evidence unless a substantial right of the party is affected, and

(1)   *Objection.* In case the ruling is one admitting evidence, a timely objection or motion to strike appears of record, stating the specific ground of objection, if the specific ground was not apparent from the context; or

(2)   *Offer of proof.* In case the ruling is one excluding evidence, the substance of the evidence was made known to the court by offer or was apparent from the context within which questions were asked.

Once the court makes a definitive ruling on the record admitting or excluding evidence, either at or before trial, a party need not renew an objection or offer of proof to preserve a claim of error for appeal.

(b)   *Record of offer and ruling.* The court may add any other or further statement which shows the character of the evidence, the form in which it was offered, the objection made, and the ruling thereon. It may direct the making of an offer in question and answer form.

(c)   *Hearing of jury.* In jury cases, proceedings shall be conducted, to the extent practicable, so as to prevent inadmissible evidence from being suggested to the jury by any means, such as making statements or offers of proof or asking questions in the hearing of the jury.

(d)   *Plain error.* Nothing in this rule precludes taking notice of plain errors affecting substantial rights although they were not brought to the attention of the court.

Rule 104 Preliminary Questions

(a)   *Questions of admissibility generally.* Preliminary questions concerning the qualification of a person to be a witness, the existence of a privilege, or the admissibility of evidence shall be determined by the court, subject to the provisions of subdivision (b). In making its determination it is not bound by the Rules of Evidence except those with respect to privileges.

(b)   *Relevancy conditioned on fact.* When the relevancy of evidence depends upon the fulfillment of a condition of fact, the court shall admit it upon, or subject to, the introduction of evidence sufficient to support a finding of the fulfillment of the condition.

(c)   *Hearing of jury.* Hearings on the admissibility of confessions shall in all cases be conducted out of the hearing of the jury. Hearings on other preliminary matters shall be so conducted when the interests of justice require, or when an accused is a witness, and so requests.

(d)   *Testimony by accused.* The accused does not, by testifying upon a preliminary matter, become subject to cross-examination as to other issues in the case.

(e)   *Weight and credibility.* This rule does not limit the right of a party to introduce before the jury evidence relevant to weight or credibility.

Rule 105 Limited Admissibility

When evidence which is admissible as to one party or for one purpose but not admissible as to another party or for another purpose is admitted, the court, upon request, shall restrict the evidence to its proper scope and instruct the jury accordingly.

Rule 106 Remainder of or Related Writings or Recorded Statements

When a writing or recorded statement or part thereof is introduced by a party, an adverse party may require the introduction at that time of any other part or any other writing or recorded statement which ought in fairness to be considered contemporaneously with it.

Rule 201 Judicial Notice of Adjudicative Facts

(a)   *Scope of rule.* This rule governs only judicial notice of adjudicative facts, and does not preclude judicial notice of legislative facts.

(b)   *Kinds of facts.* A judicially noticed fact must be one not subject to reasonable dispute in that it is either (1) generally known within the territorial jurisdiction of the trial court or (2) capable of accurate and ready determination by resort to sources whose accuracy cannot reasonably be questioned.

(c)   *When discretionary.* A court may take judicial notice, whether requested or not, and may require a party to supply necessary information.

(d)   *Opportunity to be heard.* A party is entitled upon timely request to an opportunity to be heard as to the propriety of taking judicial notice and the tenor of the matter noticed. In the absence of prior notification, the request may be made after judicial notice has been taken.

(e)   *Time of taking notice.* Judicial notice may be taken at any stage of the proceeding.

(f)   *Instructing jury.* In a civil action or proceeding, the court shall instruct the jury to accept as conclusive any fact judicially noticed. In a criminal case, the court shall instruct the jury that it may, but is not required to, accept as conclusive any fact judicially noticed.

Rule 202 Judicial Notice of Law

(a)   *When discretionary.* A court may take judicial notice without request by a party of (1) the common law, constitutions, and public statutes in force in every state, territory, and jurisdiction of the United States; (2) private acts and resolutions of the Congress of the United States and of the Legislature of Michigan, and ordinances and regulations of governmental subdivisions or agencies of Michigan; and (3) the laws of foreign countries.

(b)   *When conditionally mandatory.* A court shall take judicial notice of each matter specified in paragraph (a) of this rule if a party requests it and (1) furnishes the court sufficient information to enable it properly to comply with the request and (2) has given each adverse party such notice as the court may require to enable the adverse party to prepare to meet the request.

Rule 301 Presumptions in Civil Actions and Proceedings

In all civil actions and proceedings not otherwise provided for by statute or by these rules, a presumption imposes on the party against whom it is directed the burden of going forward with evidence to rebut or meet the presumption, but does not shift to such party the burden of proof in the sense of the risk of nonpersuasion, which remains throughout the trial upon the party on whom it was originally cast.

Rule 302 Presumptions in Criminal Cases

(a)   *Scope.* In criminal cases, presumptions against an accused, recognized at common law or created by statute, including statutory provisions that certain facts are prima facie evidence of other facts or of guilt, are governed by this rule.

(b)   *Instructing the jury.* Whenever the existence of a presumed fact against an accused is submitted to the jury, the court shall instruct the jury that it may, but need not, infer the existence of the presumed fact from the basic facts and that the prosecution still bears the burden of proof beyond a reasonable doubt of all the elements of the offense.

Rule 401 Definition of "Relevant Evidence"

"Relevant evidence" means evidence having any tendency to make the existence of any fact that is of consequence to the determination of the action more probable or less probable than it would be without the evidence.

Rule 402 Relevant Evidence Generally Admissible; Irrelevant Evidence Inadmissible

All relevant evidence is admissible, except as otherwise provided by the Constitution of the United States, the Constitution of the State of Michigan, these rules, or other rules adopted by the Supreme Court. Evidence which is not relevant is not admissible.

Rule 403 Exclusion of Relevant Evidence on Grounds of Prejudice, Confusion, or Waste of Time

Although relevant, evidence may be excluded if its probative value is substantially outweighed by the danger of unfair prejudice, confusion of the issues, or misleading the jury, or by considerations of undue delay, waste of time, or needless presentation of cumulative evidence.

Rule 404 Character Evidence Not Admissible to Prove Conduct; Exceptions; Other Crimes

(a) *Character evidence generally.* Evidence of a person's character or a trait of character is not admissible for the purpose of proving action in conformity therewith on a particular occasion, except:

(1) Character of accused. Evidence of a pertinent trait of character offered by an accused, or by the prosecution to rebut the same; or if evidence of a trait of character of the alleged victim of the crime is offered by the accused and admitted under subdivision (a)(2), evidence of a trait of character for aggression of the accused offered by the prosecution;

(2) *Character of alleged victim of homicide.* When self-defense is an issue in a charge of homicide, evidence of a trait of character for aggression of the alleged victim of the crime offered by an accused, or evidence offered by the prosecution to rebut the same, or evidence of a character trait of peacefulness of the alleged victim offered by the prosecution in a charge of homicide to rebut evidence that the alleged victim was the first aggressor;

(3) *Character of alleged victim of sexual conduct crime.* In a prosecution for criminal sexual conduct, evidence of the alleged victim's past sexual conduct with the defendant and evidence of specific

instances of sexual activity showing the source or origin of semen, pregnancy, or disease;

(4)   *Character of witness.* Evidence of the character of a witness, as provided in Rules 607, 608, and 609.

(b) *Other crimes, wrongs, or acts.*

(1)   Evidence of other crimes, wrongs, or acts is not admissible to prove the character of a person in order to show action in conformity therewith. It may, however, be admissible for other purposes, such as proof of motive, opportunity, intent, preparation, scheme, plan, or system in doing an act, knowledge, identity, or absence of mistake or accident when the same is material, whether such other crimes, wrongs, or acts are contemporaneous with, or prior or subsequent to the conduct at issue in the case.

(2)   The prosecution in a criminal case shall provide written notice at least 14 days in advance of trial, or orally on the record later if the court excuses pretrial notice on good cause shown, of the general nature of any such evidence it intends to introduce at trial and the rationale, whether or not mentioned in subparagraph (b)(1), for admitting the evidence. If necessary to a
determination of the admissibility of the evidence under this rule, the defendant shall be required to state the theory or theories of defense, limited only by the defendant's privilege against self-incrimination.

Rule 405 Methods of Proving Character

(a)   *Reputation or opinion.* In all cases in which evidence of character or a trait of character of a person is admissible, proof may be made by testimony as to reputation or by testimony in the form of an opinion. On cross-examination, inquiry is allowable into reports of relevant specific instances of conduct.

(b)   *Specific instances of conduct.* In cases in which character or a trait of character of a person is an essential element of a charge, claim, or defense, proof may also be made of specific instances of that person's conduct.

Rule 406 Habit; Routine Practice

Evidence of the habit of a person or of the routine practice of an organization, whether corroborated or not and regardless of the presence of eyewitnesses, is relevant to prove that the conduct of the person or organization on a particular occasion was in conformity with the habit or routine practice.

Rule 407 Subsequent Remedial Measures

When, after an event, measures are taken which, if taken previously, would have made the event less likely to occur, evidence of the subsequent measures is not admissible to prove negligence or culpable conduct in connection with the event. This rule does not require the exclusion of evidence of subsequent measures when offered for another purpose, such as proving ownership, control, or feasibility of precautionary measures, if controverted, or impeachment.

Rule 408 Compromise and Offers to Compromise

Evidence of (1) furnishing or offering or promising to furnish, or (2) accepting or offering or promising to accept, a valuable consideration in compromising or attempting to compromise a claim which was disputed as to either validity or amount, is not admissible to prove liability for or invalidity of the claim or its amount. Evidence of conduct or statements made in compromise negotiations is likewise not admissible. This rule does not require the exclusion of any evidence otherwise discoverable merely because it is presented in the course of compromise negotiations. This rule also does not require exclusion when the evidence is offered for another purpose, such as proving bias or prejudice of a witness, negativing a contention of undue delay, or proving an effort to obstruct a criminal investigation or prosecution.

Rule 409 Payment of Medical and Similar Expenses

Evidence of furnishing or offering or promising to pay medical, hospital, or similar expenses occasioned by an injury is not admissible to prove liability for the injury.

Rule 410 Inadmissibility of Pleas, Plea Discussions, and Related Statements

Except as otherwise provided in this rule, evidence of the following is not, in any civil or criminal proceeding, admissible against the defendant who made the plea or was a participant in the plea discussions:

(1) A plea of guilty which was later withdrawn;

(2) A plea of nolo contendere, except that, to the extent that evidence of a guilty plea would be admissible, evidence of a plea of nolo contendere to a criminal charge may be admitted in a civil proceeding to support a defense against a claim asserted by the person who entered the plea;

(3) Any statement made in the course of any proceedings under MCR 6.302 or comparable state or federal procedure regarding either of the foregoing pleas; or

(4) Any statement made in the course of plea discussions with an attorney for the prosecuting authority which do not result in a plea of guilty or which result in a plea of guilty later withdrawn.

However, such a statement is admissible (i) in any proceeding wherein another statement made in the course of the same plea or plea discussions has been introduced and the statement ought in fairness be considered contemporaneously with it, or (ii) in a criminal proceeding for perjury or false statement if the statement was made by the defendant under oath, on the record and in the presence of counsel.

Rule 411 Liability Insurance

Evidence that a person was or was not insured against liability is not admissible upon the issue whether the person acted negligently or otherwise wrongfully. This rule does not require the exclusion of evidence of insurance against liability when offered for another purpose, such as proof of agency, ownership, or control, if controverted, or bias or prejudice of a witness.

RULE 501

Rule 501 Privilege; General Rule

Privilege is governed by the common law, except as modified by statute or court rule.

RULES 601-615

Rule 601 Witnesses; General Rule of Competency

Unless the court finds after questioning a person that the person does not have sufficient physical or mental capacity or sense of obligation to testify truthfully and understandably, every person is competent to be a witness except as otherwise provided in these rules.

Rule 602 Lack of Personal Knowledge

A witness may not testify to a matter unless evidence is introduced sufficient to support a finding that the witness has personal knowledge of the matter. Evidence to prove personal knowledge may, but need not, consist of the witness' own testimony. This rule is subject to the provisions of Rule 703, relating to opinion testimony by expert witnesses.

Rule 603 Oath or Affirmation

Before testifying, every witness shall be required to declare that the witness will testify truthfully, by oath or affirmation administered in a form calculated to awaken the witness' conscience and impress the witness' mind with the duty to do so.

Rule 604 Interpreters

An interpreter is subject to the provisions of these rules relating to qualification as an expert and the administration of an oath or affirmation to make a true translation.

Rule 605 Competency of Judge as Witness

The judge presiding at the trial may not testify in that trial as a witness. No objection need be made in order to preserve the point.

Rule 606 Competency of Juror as Witness

(a)   At the trial. A member of the jury may not testify as a witness before that jury in the trial of the case in which the juror is sitting. No objection need be made in order to preserve the point.

(b)   Inquiry into validity of verdict or indictment. Upon an inquiry into the validity of a verdict or indictment, a juror may not testify as to any matter or statement occurring during the course of the jury's deliberations or to the effect of anything upon that or any other juror's mind or emotions as influencing the juror to assent

to or dissent from the verdict or indictment or concerning the juror's mental processes in connection therewith. But a juror may testify about (1) whether extraneous prejudicial information was improperly brought to the jury's attention, (2) whether any outside influence was improperly brought to bear upon any juror, or (3) whether there was a mistake in entering the verdict onto the verdict form. A juror's affidavit or evidence of any statement by the juror may not be received on a matter about which the juror would be precluded from testifying.

Rule 607 Who May Impeach

The credibility of a witness may be attacked by any party, including the party calling the witness.

Rule 608 Evidence of Character and Conduct of Witness

(a)   *Opinion and reputation evidence of character.* The credibility of a witness may be attacked or supported by evidence in the form of opinion or reputation, but subject to these limitations: (1) the evidence may refer only to character for truthfulness or untruthfulness, and (2) evidence of truthful character is admissible only after the character of the witness for truthfulness has been attacked by opinion or reputation evidence or otherwise.

(b)   *Specific instances of conduct.* Specific instances of the conduct of a witness, for the purpose of attacking or supporting the witness' credibility, other than conviction of crime as provided in Rule 609, may not be proved by extrinsic evidence. They may, however, in the discretion of the court, if probative of truthfulness or untruthfulness, be inquired into on cross-examination of the witness (1) concerning the witness' character for truthfulness or untruthfulness, or (2) concerning the character for truthfulness or untruthfulness of another witness as to which character the witness being cross-examined has testified.

The giving of testimony, whether by an accused or by any other witness, does not operate as a waiver of the accused's or the witness' privilege against selfincrimination when examined with respect to matters which relate only to credibility.

Rule 609 Impeachment by Evidence of Conviction of Crime

(a)   *General rule.* For the purpose of attacking the credibility of a witness, evidence that the witness has been convicted of a crime shall not be admitted unless the evidence has been elicited from the witness or established by public record during cross-examination, and

   (1) the crime contained an element of dishonesty or false statement, or

   (2) the crime contained an element of theft, and

      (A)   the crime was punishable by imprisonment in excess of one year or death under the law under which the witness was convicted, and

(B)   the court determines that the evidence has significant probative value on the issue of credibility and, if the witness is the defendant in a criminal trial, the court further determines that the probative value of the evidence outweighs its prejudicial effect.

(b)   *Determining probative value and prejudicial effect.* For purposes of the probative value determination required by subrule (a)(2)(B), the court shall consider only the age of the conviction and the degree to which a conviction of the crime is indicative of veracity. If a determination of prejudicial effect is required, the court shall consider only the conviction's similarity to the charged offense and the possible effects on the decisional process if admitting the evidence causes the defendant to elect not to testify. The court must articulate, on the record, the analysis of each factor.

(c)   *Time limit.* Evidence of a conviction under this rule is not admissible if a period of more than ten years has elapsed since the date of the conviction or of the release of the witness from the confinement imposed for that conviction, whichever is the later date.

(d)   *Effect of pardon, annulment, or certificate of rehabilitation.* Evidence of a conviction is not admissible under this rule if (1) the conviction has been the subject of a pardon, annulment, certificate of rehabilitation, or other equivalent procedure based on a finding of the rehabilitation of the person convicted, and that person has not been convicted of a subsequent crime which was punishable by death or imprisonment in excess of one year, or (2) the conviction has been the subject of a pardon, annulment, or other equivalent procedure based on a finding of innocence.

(e)   *Juvenile adjudications.* Evidence of juvenile adjudications is generally not admissible under this rule, except in subsequent cases against the same child in the juvenile division of a probate court. The court may, however, in a criminal case or a juvenile proceeding against the child allow evidence of a juvenile adjudication of a witness other than the accused if conviction of the offense would be admissible to attack the credibility of an adult and the court is satisfied that admission is necessary for a fair determination of the case or proceeding.

(f)   *Pendency of appeal.* The pendency of an appeal therefrom does not render evidence of a conviction inadmissible. Evidence of the pendency of an appeal is admissible.

GRIFFIN, J., states: Because I disagree with the majority opinion in *People v Allen,* [429 Mich 558 (1988)] I dissent from the adoption of this amendment of MRE 609.

Rule 610 Religious Beliefs or Opinions

Evidence of the beliefs or opinions of a witness on matters of religion is not admissible for the purpose of showing that by reason of their nature the witness' credibility is impaired or enhanced.

Rule 611 Mode and Order of Interrogation and Presentation

(a) *Control by court.* The court shall exercise reasonable control over the mode and order of interrogating witnesses and presenting evidence so as to (1) make the interrogation and presentation effective for the ascertainment of the truth, (2) avoid needless consumption of time, and (3) protect witnesses from harassment or undue embarrassment.

(b) Appearance of Parties and Witnesses. The court shall exercise reasonable control over the appearance of parties and witnesses so as to (1) ensure that the demeanor of such persons may be observed and assessed by the fact-finder and (2) ensure the accurate identification of such persons.

(c) *Scope of cross-examination.* A witness may be cross-examined on any matter relevant to any issue in the case, including credibility. The judge may limit crossexamination with respect to matters not testified to on direct examination.

(d) *Leading Questions.*

   (1) Leading questions should not be used on the direct examination of a witness except as may be necessary to develop the witness' testimony.

   (2) Ordinarily leading questions should be permitted on cross-examination.

   (3) When a party calls a hostile witness, an adverse party or a witness identified with an adverse party, interrogation may be by leading questions. It is not necessary to declare the intent to ask leading questions before the questioning begins or before the questioning moves beyond preliminary inquiries.

Rule 612 Writing or Object Used to Refresh Memory

(a)   *While testifying.* If, while testifying, a witness uses a writing or object to refresh memory, an adverse party is entitled to have the writing or object produced at the trial, hearing, or deposition in which the witness is testifying.

(b)   *Before testifying.* If, before testifying, a witness uses a writing or object to refresh memory for the purpose of testifying and the court in its discretion determines that the interests of justice so require, an adverse party is entitled to have the writing or object produced, if practicable, at the trial, hearing, or deposition in which the witness is testifying.

(c)   *Terms and conditions of production and use.* A party entitled to have a writing or object produced under this rule is entitled to inspect it, to cross-examine the witness thereon, and to introduce in evidence, for their bearing on credibility only unless otherwise admissible under these rules for another purpose, those portions which relate to the testimony of the witness. If production of the writing or object at the trial, hearing, or deposition is impracticable, the court may order it made available for inspection. If it is claimed that the writing or object contains matters not related to the subject matter of the testimony the court shall examine the writing or object in camera, excise any portions not so related, and order delivery of the remainder to the party entitled thereto. Any portion withheld over objections shall be preserved and made available to the appellate court in the event of an appeal. If a writing or object is not produced, made available for inspection, or delivered pursuant to order under this rule, the court shall make any order justice requires, except that in criminal cases when the prosecution elects not to comply, the order shall be one striking the testimony or, if the court in its discretion determines that the interests of justice so require, declaring a mistrial.

Rule 613 Prior Statements of Witnesses

(a)   *Examining witness concerning prior statement.* In examining a witness concerning a prior statement made by the witness, whether written or not, the statement need not be shown nor its contents disclosed to the witness at that time, but on request it shall be shown or disclosed to opposing counsel and the witness.

(b)   *Extrinsic evidence of prior inconsistent statement of witness.* Extrinsic evidence of a prior inconsistent statement by a witness is not admissible unless the witness is afforded an opportunity to explain or deny the same and the opposite party is afforded an opportunity to interrogate the witness thereon, or the interests of justice otherwise require. This provision does not apply to admissions of a partyopponent as defined in Rule 801(d)(2).

Rule 614 Calling and Interrogation of Witnesses by Court

(a)   *Calling by court.* The court may, on its own motion or at the suggestion of a party, call witnesses, and all parties are entitled to cross-examine witnesses thus called.

(b)   *Interrogation by court.* The court may interrogate witnesses, whether called by itself or by a party.

(c)   *Objections.* Objections to the calling of witnesses by the court or to interrogation by it may be made at the time or at the next available opportunity when the jury is not present.

Rule 615 Exclusion of Witnesses

At the request of a party the court may order witnesses excluded so that they cannot hear the testimony of other witnesses, and it may make the order of its own motion. This rule does not authorize exclusion of (1) a party who is a natural person, or (2) an officer or employee of a party which is not a natural person designated as its representative by its attorney, or (3) a person whose presence is shown by a party to be essential to the presentation of the party's cause.

Rule 701 Opinion Testimony by Lay Witnesses

If the witness is not testifying as an expert, the witness' testimony in the form of opinions or inferences is limited to those opinions or inferences which are (a) rationally based on the perception of the witness and (b) helpful to a clear understanding of the witness' testimony or the determination of a fact in issue.

Rule 702 Testimony by Experts

If the court determines that scientific, technical, or other specialized knowledge will assist the trier of fact to understand the evidence or to determine a fact in issue, a witness qualified as an expert by knowledge, skill, experience, training, or education may testify thereto in the form of an opinion or otherwise if (1) the testimony is based on sufficient facts or data, (2) the testimony is the product of reliable principles and methods, and (3) the witness has applied the principles and methods reliably to the facts of the case.

Rule 703 Bases of Opinion Testimony by Experts

The facts or data in the particular case upon which an expert bases an opinion or inference shall be in evidence. This rule does not restrict the discretion of the court to receive expert opinion testimony subject to the condition that the factual bases of the opinion be admitted in evidence hereafter.

Rule 704 Opinion on Ultimate Issue

Testimony in the form of an opinion or inference otherwise admissible is not objectionable because it embraces an ultimate issue to be decided by the trier of fact.

Rule 705 Disclosure of Facts or Data Underlying Expert Opinion

The expert may testify in terms of opinion or inference and give reasons therefor without prior disclosure of the underlying facts or data, unless the court requires otherwise. The expert may in any event be required to disclose the underlying facts or data on cross-examination.

Rule 706 Court-Appointed Experts

(a) *Appointment.* The court may on its own motion or on the motion of any party enter an order to show cause why expert witnesses should not be appointed, and may request the parties to submit nominations. The court may appoint any expert witnesses agreed upon by the parties, and may appoint expert witnesses of its own selection. An expert witness shall not be appointed by the court unless the witness consents to act. A witness so appointed shall be informed of the witness' duties by the court in writing, a copy of which shall be filed with the clerk, or at a conference in which the parties shall have opportunity to participate. A witness so appointed shall advise the parties of the witness' findings, if any; the witness' deposition may be taken by any party; and the witness may be called to testify by the court or any party. The witness shall be subject to cross-examination by each party, including a party calling the witness.

(b)   *Compensation.* Expert witnesses so appointed are entitled to reasonable compensation in whatever sum the court may allow. The compensation thus fixed is payable from funds which may be provided by law in criminal cases and civil actions and proceedings involving just compensation under the Fifth Amendment. In other civil actions and proceedings the compensation shall be paid by the parties in such proportion and at such time as the court directs, and thereafter charged in like manner as other costs.

(c)   *Disclosure of appointment.* In the exercise of its discretion, the court may authorize disclosure to the jury of the fact that the court appointed the expert witness.

(d)   *Parties' experts of own selection.* Nothing in this rule limits the parties in calling expert witnesses of their own selection.

Rule 707 Use of Learned Treatises for Impeachment

To the extent called to the attention of an expert witness upon cross-examination, statements contained in published treatises, periodicals, or pamphlets on a subject of history, medicine, or other science or art, established as a reliable authority by the testimony or admission of the witness or by other expert testimony or by judicial notice, are admissible for impeachment purposes only. If admitted, the statements may be read into evidence but may not be received as exhibits.

RULES 801-806

Rule 801 Hearsay; Definitions

The following definitions apply under this article:

(a) *Statement.* A "statement" is (1) an oral or written assertion or (2) nonverbal conduct of a person, if it is intended by the person as an assertion.

(b) *Declarant.* A "declarant" is a person who makes a statement.

(c) *Hearsay.* "Hearsay" is a statement, other than the one made by the declarant while testifying at the trial or hearing, offered in evidence to prove the truth of the matter asserted.

(d) *Statements which are not hearsay.* A statement is not hearsay if–

(1)   *Prior statement of witness.* The declarant testifies at the trial or hearing and is subject to cross-examination concerning the statement, and the statement is (A) inconsistent with the declarant's testimony, and was given under oath subject to the penalty of perjury at a trial, hearing, or other proceeding, or in a deposition, or (B) consistent with the declarant's testimony and is offered to rebut an express or implied charge against the declarant of recent fabrication or improper influence or motive, or (C) one of identification of a person made after perceiving the person; or

(2)   *Admission by party-opponent.* The statement is offered against a party and is (A) the party's own statement, in either an individual or a representative capacity, except statements made in connection with a guilty plea to a misdemeanor motor vehicle violation or an admission of responsibility for a civil infraction under laws pertaining to motor vehicles, or (B) a statement of which the party has manifested an adoption or belief in its truth, or (C) a statement by a person authorized by the party to make a statement concerning the subject, or (D) a statement by the party's agent or servant concerning a matter within the scope of the agency or employment, made during the existence of the relationship, or (E) a statement by a coconspirator of a party during the course and in furtherance of the conspiracy on independent proof of the conspiracy.

Rule 802 Hearsay Rule

Hearsay is not admissible except as provided by these rules.

Rule 803 Hearsay Exceptions; Availability of Declarant Immaterial

The following are not excluded by the hearsay rule, even though the declarant is available as a witness:

(1)   *Present sense impression.* A statement describing or explaining an event or condition made while the declarant was perceiving the event or condition, or immediately thereafter.

(2)   *Excited utterance.* A statement relating to a startling event or condition made while the declarant was under the stress of excitement caused by the event or condition.

(3)   *Then existing mental, emotional, or physical condition.* A statement of the declarant's then existing state of mind, emotion, sensation, or physical condition (such as intent, plan, motive, design, mental feeling, pain, and bodily health), but not including a statement of memory or belief to prove the fact remembered or believed unless it relates to the execution, revocation, identification, or terms of declarant's will.

(4)   *Statements made for purposes of medical treatment or medical diagnosis in connection with treatment.* Statements made for purposes of medical treatment or medical diagnosis in connection with treatment and describing medical history, or past or present symptoms, pain, or sensations, or the inception or general character of the cause or external source thereof insofar as reasonably necessary to such diagnosis and treatment.

(5)   *Recorded recollection.* A memorandum or record concerning a matter about which a witness once had knowledge but now has insufficient recollection to enable the witness to testify fully and accurately, shown to have been made or adopted by the witness when the matter was fresh in the witness' memory and to reflect that knowledge correctly. If admitted, the memorandum or record may be read into evidence but may not itself be received as an exhibit unless offered by an adverse party.

(6)   *Records of regularly conducted activity.* A memorandum, report, record, or data compilation, in any form, of acts, transactions, occurrences, events, conditions, opinions, or diagnoses, made at or near the time by, or from information transmitted by, a person with knowledge, if kept in the course of a regularly conducted business activity, and if it was the regular practice of that business activity to make the memorandum, report, record, or data compilation, all as shown by the testimony of the custodian or other qualified witness, or by certification that complies with a rule promulgated by the supreme court or a statute permitting certification, unless the source of information or the method or circumstances of preparation indicate lack of trustworthiness. The term "business" as used in this paragraph includes business, institution, association, profession, occupation, and calling of every kind, whether or not conducted for profit.

(7)   *Absence of entry in records kept in accordance with the provisions of paragraph (6).* Evidence that a matter is not included in the memoranda, reports, records, or data compilations, in any form, kept in accordance with

the provisions of paragraph (6), to prove the nonoccurrence or nonexistence of the matter, if the matter was of a kind of which a memorandum, report, record, or data compilation was regularly made and preserved, unless the sources of information or other circumstances indicate lack of trustworthiness.

(8)   *Public records and reports.* Records, reports, statements, or data compilations, in any form, of public offices or agencies, setting forth (A) the activities of the office or agency, or (B) matters observed pursuant to duty imposed by law as to which matters there was a duty to report, excluding, however, in criminal cases matters observed by police officers and other law enforcement personnel, and subject to the limitations of MCL 257.624.

(9)   *Records of vital statistics.* Records or data compilations, in any form, of births, fetal deaths, deaths, or marriages, if the report thereof was made to a public office pursuant to requirements of law.

(10)   *Absence of public record or entry.* To prove the absence of a record, report, statement, or data compilation, in any form, or the nonoccurrence or nonexistence of a matter of which a record, report, statement, or data compilation, in any form, was regularly made and preserved by a public office or agency, evidence in the form of a certification in accordance with Rule 902, or testimony, that diligent search failed to disclose the record, report, statement, or data compilation, or entry.

(11)   *Records of religious organizations.* Statements of births, marriages, divorces, deaths, legitimacy, ancestry, relationship by blood or marriage, or other similar facts of personal or family history, contained in a regularly kept record of a religious organization.

(12)   *Marriage, baptismal, and similar certificates.* Statements of fact contained in a certificate that the maker performed a marriage or other ceremony or administered a sacrament, made by a member of the clergy, public official, or other person authorized by the rules or practices of a religious organization or by law to perform the act certified, and purporting to have been issued at the time of the act or within a reasonable time thereafter.

(13)   *Family records.* Statements of fact concerning personal or family history contained in family Bibles, genealogies, charts, engravings on rings, inscriptions on family portraits, engravings on urns, crypts, or tombstones, or the like.

(14)   *Records of documents affecting an interest in property.* The record of a document purporting to establish or affect an interest in property, as proof of the content of the original recorded document and its execution and delivery by each person by whom it purports to have been executed, if the record is a record of a public office and an applicable statute authorizes the recording of documents of that kind in that office.

(15) *Statements in documents affecting an interest in property.* A statement contained in a document purporting to establish or affect an interest in property if the matter stated was relevant to the purpose of the document, unless dealings with the property since the document was made have been inconsistent with the truth of the statement or the purport of the document.

(16) *Statements in ancient documents.* Statements in a document in existence twenty years or more the authenticity of which is established.

(17) *Market reports, commercial publications.* Market quotations, tabulations, lists, directories, or other published compilations, generally used and relied upon by the public or by persons in particular occupations.

(18) *Deposition testimony of an expert.* Testimony given as a witness in a deposition taken in compliance with law in the course of the same proceeding if the court finds that the deponent is an expert witness and if the deponent is not a party to the proceeding.

(19) *Reputation concerning personal or family history.* Reputation among members of a person's family by blood, adoption, or marriage, or among a person's associates, or in the community, concerning a person's birth, adoption, marriage, divorce, death, legitimacy, relationship by blood, adoption, or marriage, ancestry, or other similar fact of personal or family history.

(20) *Reputation concerning boundaries or general history.* Reputation in a community, arising before the controversy, as to boundaries of or customs affecting lands in the community, and reputation as to events of general history important to the community or state or nation in which located.

(21) *Reputation as to character.* Reputation of a person's character among associates or in the community.

(22) *Judgment of previous conviction.* Evidence of a final judgment, entered after a trial or upon a plea of guilty (or upon a plea of nolo contendere if evidence of the plea is not excluded by MRE 410), adjudging a person guilty of a crime punishable by death or imprisonment in excess of one year, to prove any fact essential to sustain the judgment, but not including, when offered by the state in a criminal prosecution for purposes other than impeachment, judgments against persons other than the accused. The pendency of an appeal may be shown but does not affect admissibility.

(23) *Judgment as to personal, family, or general history, or boundaries.* Judgments as proof of matters of personal, family or general history, or boundaries, essential to the judgment, if the same would be provable by evidence of reputation.

(24) *Other Exceptions.* A statement not specifically covered by any of the foregoing exceptions but having equivalent circumstantial guarantees of

trustworthiness, if the court determines that (A) the statement is offered as evidence of a material fact, (B) the statement is more probative on the point for which it is offered than any other evidence that the proponent can procure through reasonable efforts, and (C) the general purposes of these rules and the interests of justice will best be served by admission of the statement into evidence. However, a statement may not be admitted under this exception unless the proponent of the statement makes known to the adverse party, sufficiently in advance of the trial or hearing to provide the adverse party with a fair opportunity to prepare to meet it, the proponent's intention to offer the statement and the particulars of it, including the name and address of the declarant.

Rule 803A Hearsay Exception; Child's Statement About Sexual Act

A statement describing an incident that included a sexual act performed with or on the declarant by the defendant or an accomplice is admissible to the extent that it corroborates testimony given by the declarant during the same proceeding, provided:

(1) the declarant was under the age of ten when the statement was made;

(2) the statement is shown to have been spontaneous and without indication of manufacture;

(3) either the declarant made the statement immediately after the incident or any delay is excusable as having been caused by fear or other equally effective circumstance; and

(4) the statement is introduced through the testimony of someone other than the declarant.

If the declarant made more than one corroborative statement about the incident, only the first is admissible under this rule.

A statement may not be admitted under this rule unless the proponent of the statement makes known to the adverse party the intent to offer the statement, and the particulars of the statement, sufficiently in advance of the trial or hearing to provide the adverse party with a fair opportunity to prepare to meet the statement.

This rule applies in criminal and delinquency proceedings only.

Rule 804 Hearsay Exceptions; Declarant Unavailable

(a) *Definition of unavailability.* "Unavailability as a witness" includes situations in which the declarant–

(1) is exempted by ruling of the court on the ground of privilege from testifying concerning the subject matter of the declarant's statement; or

(2) persists in refusing to testify concerning the subject matter of the declarant's statement despite an order of the court to do so; or

(3) has a lack of memory of the subject matter of the declarant's statement; or

(4) is unable to be present or to testify at the hearing because of death or then existing physical or mental illness or infirmity; or

(5) is absent from the hearing and the proponent of a statement has been unable to procure the declarant's attendance (or in the case of a hearsay exception under subdivision (b)(2), (3), or (4), the declarant's attendance or testimony) by process or other reasonable means, and in a criminal case, due diligence is shown.

A declarant is not unavailable as a witness if exemption, refusal, claim of lack of memory, inability, or absence is due to the procurement or wrongdoing of the proponent of a statement for the purpose of preventing the witness from attending or testifying.

(b) *Hearsay exceptions.* The following are not excluded by the hearsay rule if the declarant is unavailable as a witness:

(1)   *Former testimony.* Testimony given as a witness at another hearing of the same or a different proceeding, if the party against whom the testimony is now offered, or, in a civil action or proceeding, a predecessor in interest, had an opportunity and similar motive to develop the testimony by direct, cross, or redirect examination.

(2)   *Statement under belief of impending death.* In a prosecution for homicide or in a civil action or proceeding, a statement made by a declarant while believing that the declarant's death was imminent, concerning the cause or circumstances of what the declarant believed to be impending death.

(3)   *Statement against interest.* A statement which was at the time of its making so far contrary to the declarant's pecuniary or proprietary interest, or so far tended to subject the declarant to civil or criminal liability, or to render invalid a claim by the declarant against another, that a reasonable person in the declarant's position would not have made the statement unless believing it to be true. A statement tending to expose the declarant to criminal liability and offered to exculpate the accused is not admissible unless corroborating circumstances clearly indicate the trustworthiness of the statement.

(4)   *Statement of personal or family history.* (A) A statement concerning the declarant's own birth, adoption, marriage, divorce, legitimacy, relationship by blood, adoption, or marriage, ancestry, or other similar fact of personal or family history, even though declarant had no means of acquiring personal knowledge of the matter stated; or

(B) a statement concerning the foregoing matters, and death also, of another person, if the declarant was related to the other by blood, adoption, or marriage or was so intimately associated with the other's family as to be likely to have accurate information concerning the matter declared.

(5)   *Deposition Testimony.* Testimony given as a witness in a deposition taken in compliance with law in the course of the same or another proceeding, if the party against whom the testimony is now offered, or, in a civil action or proceeding, a predecessor in interest, had an opportunity and similar motive to develop the testimony by direct, cross, or redirect examination.

For purposes of this subsection only, "unavailability of a witness" also includes situations in which:

(A)   The witness is at a greater distance than 100 miles from the place of trial or hearing, or is out of the United States, unless it appears that the absence of the witness was procured by the party offering the deposition; or

(B)   On motion and notice, such exceptional circumstances exist as to make it desirable, in the interests of justice, and with due regard to the importance of presenting the testimony of witnesses orally in open court, to allow the deposition to be used.

(6)   *Statement by declarant made unavailable by opponent.* A statement offered against a party that has engaged in or encouraged wrongdoing that was intended to, and did, procure the unavailability of the declarant as a witness.

(7)   *Other Exceptions.* A statement not specifically covered by any of the foregoing exceptions but having equivalent circumstantial guarantees of trustworthiness, if the court determines that (A) the statement is offered as evidence of a material fact, (B) the statement is more probative on the point for which it is offered than any other evidence that the proponent can procure through reasonable efforts, and (C) the general purposes of these rules and the interests of justice will best be served by admission of the statement into evidence. However, a statement may not be admitted under this exception unless the proponent of the statement makes known to the adverse party, sufficiently in advance of the trial or hearing to provide the adverse party with a fair opportunity to prepare to meet it, the proponent's intention to offer the statement and the particulars of it, including the name and address of the declarant.

MRE 804 is identical with Rule 804 of the Federal Rules of Evidence except:

(1)   MRE 804(a)(3) is identical with Federal Rule 804(a)(3) except that the word "has" is substituted for the phrase "testifies to."

(2)   MRE 804(a)(5) is identical with Federal Rule 804(a)(5) except for the addition of the phrase: "and in a criminal case, due diligence is shown."

(3)   MRE 804(b)(3) is identical with Federal Rule 804(b)(3) except that the phrase "reasonable person" is substituted for the phrase "reasonable man."

(4)   The Michigan Rules of Evidence contain no catch-all hearsay exception such as found in Federal Rule 804(b)(5).

(5)   Subrule (b)(5) defines several hearsay exceptions for deposition testimony. The new subrule combines a part of former subrule (b)(1) with parts of former MCR 2.308(A), which has been amended concurrently.

Note to amendment of January 19, 1996:

The 1996 adoption of MRE 804(b)(6) incorporated into the Michigan Rules of Evidence the residual or "catch-all" exceptions to the hearsay rule that are part of the Federal Rules of Evidence.

Note to amendment of May 21, 2001:

MRE 804(b)(6) was added and is almost identical to FRE 804(b)(6), which was added to the federal rules effective December 1, 1997. The new subrule creates a hearsay exception for prior statements by a witness who has become unavailable due to wrongful acts committed or encouraged by the party against whom the statement is to be introduced.

Rule 805 Hearsay Within Hearsay

Hearsay included within hearsay is not excluded under the hearsay rule if each part of the combined statements conforms with an exception to the hearsay rule provided in these rules.

Rule 806 Attacking and Supporting Credibility of Declarant

When a hearsay statement, or a statement defined in Rule 801(d)(2)(C), (D), or (E), has been admitted in evidence, the credibility of the declarant may be attacked, and if attacked may be supported, by any evidence which would be admissible for those purposes if declarant had testified as a witness. Evidence of a statement or conduct by the declarant at any time, inconsistent with the declarant's hearsay statement, is not subject to any requirement that the declarant may have been afforded an opportunity to deny or explain. If the party against whom a hearsay statement has been admitted calls the declarant as a witness, the party is entitled to examine the declarant on the statement as if under cross-examination.

Rule 901 Requirement of Authentication or Identification

(a)   *General provision.* The requirement of authentication or identification as a condition precedent to admissibility is satisfied by evidence sufficient to support a

finding that the matter in question is what its proponent claims.

(b)   *Illustrations.* By way of illustration only, and not by way of limitation, the following are examples of authentication or identification conforming with the requirements of this rule:

(1)   *Testimony of witness with knowledge.* Testimony that a matter is what it is claimed to be.

(2)   *Nonexpert opinion on handwriting.* Nonexpert opinion as to the genuineness of handwriting, based upon familiarity not acquired for purposes of the litigation.

(3)   *Comparison by trier or expert witness.* Comparison by the trier of fact or by expert witnesses with specimens which have been authenticated.

(4)   *Distinctive characteristics and the like.* Appearance, contents, substance, internal patterns, or other distinctive characteristics, taken in conjunction with circumstances.

(5)   *Voice identification.* Identification of a voice, whether heard firsthand or through mechanical or electronic transmission or recording, by opinion based upon hearing the voice at any time under circumstances connecting it with the alleged speaker.

(6)   *Telephone conversations.* Telephone conversations, by evidence that a call was made to the number assigned at the time by the telephone company to a particular person or business, if (A) in the case of a person, circumstances, including self-identification, show the person answering to be the one called, or (B) in the case of a business, the call was made to a place of business and the conversation related to business reasonably transacted over the telephone.

(7)   *Public records or reports.* Evidence that a writing authorized by law to be recorded or filed and in fact recorded or filed in a public office, or a purported public record, report, statement, or data compilation, in any form, is from the public office where items of this nature are kept.

(8)   *Ancient documents or data compilation.* Evidence that a document or data compilation, in any form, (A) is in such condition as to create no suspicion concerning its authenticity, (B) was in a place where

it, if authentic, would likely be, and (C) has been in existence 20 years or more at the time it is offered.

(9)   *Process or system.* Evidence describing a process or system used to produce a result and showing that the process or system produces an accurate result.

(10)   *Methods provided by statute or rule.* Any method of authentication or identification provided by the Supreme Court of Michigan or by a Michigan statute.

Rule 902 Self-Authentication

Extrinsic evidence of authenticity as a condition precedent to admissibility is not required with respect to the following:

(1)   *Domestic public documents under seal.* A document bearing a seal purporting to be that of the United States, or of any state, district, commonwealth, territory, or insular possession thereof, or the Panama Canal Zone, or the Trust Territory of the Pacific Islands, or of a political subdivision, department, officer, or agency thereof, and a signature purporting to be an attestation or execution.

(2)   *Domestic public documents not under seal.* A document purporting to bear the signature in the official capacity of an officer or employee of any entity included in paragraph (1) hereof, having no seal, if a public officer having a seal and having official duties in the district or political subdivision of the officer or employee certifies under seal that the signer has the official capacity and that the signature is genuine.

(3)   *Foreign public documents.* A document purporting to be executed or attested in an official capacity by a person authorized by the laws of a foreign country to make the execution or attestation, and accompanied by a final certification as to the genuineness of the signature and official position (A) of the executing or attesting person, or (B) of any foreign official whose certificate of genuineness of signature and official position relates to the execution or attestation or is in a chain of certificates of genuineness of signature and official position relating to the execution or attestation. A final certification may be made by a secretary of embassy or legation, consul general, consul, vice consul, or consular agent of the United States, or a diplomatic or consular official of the foreign country assigned or accredited to the United States. If reasonable opportunity has been given to all parties to investigate the authenticity and accuracy of official documents, the court may, for good cause shown, order that they be treated as presumptively authentic without final certification or permit them to be evidenced by an attested summary with or without final certification.

(4)   *Certified copies of public records.* A copy of an official record or report or entry therein, or of a document authorized by law to be recorded or filed

and actually recorded or filed in a public office, including data compilations in any form, certified as correct by the custodian or other person authorized to make the certification, by certificate complying with paragraph (1), (2), or (3) or complying with any law of the United States or of this state.

(5) *Official publications.* Books, pamphlets, or other publications purporting to be issued by public authority.

(6) *Newspapers and periodicals.* Printed materials purporting to be newspapers or periodicals.

(7) *Trade inscriptions and the like.* Inscriptions, signs, tags, or labels purporting to have been affixed in the course of business and indicating ownership, control, or origin.

(8) *Acknowledged documents.* Documents accompanied by a certificate of acknowledgment executed in the manner provided by law by a notary public or other officer authorized by law to take acknowledgments.

(9) *Commercial paper and related documents.* Commercial paper, signatures thereon, and documents relating thereto to the extent provided by general commercial law.

(10) *Presumptions created by law.* Any signature, document, or other matter declared by any law of the United States or of this state to be presumptively or prima facie genuine or authentic.

(11) *Certified records of regularly conducted activity.* The original or a duplicate of a record, whether domestic or foreign, of regularly conducted business activity that would be admissible under rule 803(6), if accompanied by a written declaration under oath by its custodian or other qualified person certifying that

(A) The record was made at or near the time of the occurrence of the matters set forth by, or from information transmitted by, a person with knowledge of those matters;

(B) The record was kept in the course of the regularly conducted business activity; and

(C) It was the regular practice of the business activity to make the record.

A party intending to offer a record into evidence under this paragraph must provide written notice of that intention to all adverse parties, and must make the record and declaration available for inspection sufficiently in advance of their offer into evidence to provide an adverse party with a fair opportunity to challenge them.

Rule 903 Subscribing Witness' Testimony Unnecessary

The testimony of a subscribing witness is not necessary to authenticate a writing unless required by the laws of the jurisdiction whose laws govern the validity of the writing.

RULES 1001-1008

Rule 1001 Contents of Writings, Recordings, and Photographs;

Definitions For purposes of this article the following definitions are applicable:

(1)   *Writings and recordings.* "Writings" and "recordings" consist of letters, words, or numbers, or their equivalent, set down by handwriting, typewriting, printing, photostating, photographing, magnetic impulse, mechanical or electronic recording, or other form of data compilation.

(2)   *Photographs.* "Photographs" include still photographs, x-ray films, video tapes, and motion pictures.

(3)   *Original.* An "original" of a writing or recording is the writing or recording itself or any counterpart intended to have the same effect by a person executing or issuing it. An "original" of a photograph includes the negative or any print therefrom. If data are stored in a computer or similar device, any printout or other output readable by sight, shown to reflect the data accurately, is an "original."

(4)   *Duplicate.* A "duplicate" is a counterpart produced by the same impression as the original, or from the same matrix, or by means of photography, including enlargements and miniatures, or by mechanical or electronic re-recording, or by chemical reproduction, or by other equivalent techniques, which accurately reproduces the original.

Rule 1002 Requirement of Original

To prove the content of a writing, recording, or photograph, the original writing, recording, or photograph is required, except as otherwise provided in these rules or by statute.

Rule 1003 Admissibility of Duplicates

A duplicate is admissible to the same extent as an original unless (1) a genuine question is raised as to the authenticity of the original or (2) in the circumstances it would be unfair to admit the duplicate in lieu of the original.

Rule 1004 Admissibility of Other Evidence of Contents

The original is not required, and other evidence of the contents of a writing, recording, or photograph is admissible if–

(1)   *Originals lost or destroyed.* All originals are lost or have been destroyed, unless the proponent lost or destroyed them in bad faith; or

(2)   *Original not obtainable.* No original can be obtained by any available judicial process or procedure; or

(3)   *Original in possession of opponent.* At a time when an original was under the control of the party against whom offered, that party was put on notice, by the pleadings or otherwise, that the contents would be a subject of proof at the hearing, and that party does not produce the original at the hearing; or

(4)   *Collateral matters.* The writing, recording, or photograph is not closely related to a controlling issue.

Rule 1005 Public Records

The contents of an official record, or of a document authorized to be recorded or filed and actually recorded or filed, including data compilations in any form, if otherwise admissible, may be proved by copy, certified as correct in accordance with Rule 902 or testified to be correct by a witness who has compared it with the original. If a copy which complies with the foregoing cannot be obtained by the exercise of reasonable diligence, then other evidence of the contents may be given.

Rule 1006 Summaries

The contents of voluminous writings, recordings, or photographs which cannot conveniently be examined in court may be presented in the form of a chart, summary, or calculation. The originals, or duplicates, shall be made available for examination or copying, or both, by other parties at reasonable time and place. The court may order that they be produced in court.

Rule 1007 Testimony or Written Admission of a Party

Contents of writings, recordings, or photographs may be proved by the testimony or deposition of the party against whom offered or by that party's written admission, without accounting for the nonproduction of the original.

Rule 1008 Functions of Court and Jury

When the admissibility of other evidence of contents of writings, recordings, or photographs under these rules depends upon the fulfillment of a condition of fact, the question whether the condition has been fulfilled is ordinarily for the court to determine in accordance with the provisions of Rule 104. However, when an issue is raised (a) whether the asserted writing ever existed, or (b) whether another writing, recording, or photograph produced at the trial is the original, or (c) whether other evidence of contents correctly reflects the contents, the issue is for the trier of fact to determine as in the case of other issues of fact.

Rule 1101 Applicability

(a)   *Rules applicable.* Except as otherwise provided in subdivision (b), these rules apply to all actions and proceedings in the courts of this state.

(b)   *Rules inapplicable.* The rules other than those with respect to privileges do not apply in the following situations and proceedings:

(1) *Preliminary questions of fact.* The determination of questions of fact preliminary to admissibility of evidence when the issue is to be determined by the court under Rule 104(a).

(2) *Grand jury.* Proceedings before grand juries.

(3) *Miscellaneous proceedings.* Proceedings for extradition or rendition; sentencing, or granting or revoking probation; issuance of warrants for arrest, criminal summonses, and search warrants; and proceedings with respect to release on bail or otherwise.

(4) *Contempt proceedings.* Contempt proceedings in which the court may act summarily.

(5) *Small claims.* Small claims division of the district court.

(6) *In camera custody hearings.* In camera proceedings in child custody matters to determine a child's custodial preference.

(7) *Proceedings involving juveniles.* Proceedings in the family division of the circuit court wherever MCR subchapter 3.900 states that the Michigan Rules of Evidence do not apply.

(8) *Preliminary examinations.* At preliminary examinations in criminal cases, hearsay is admissible to prove, with regard to property, the ownership, authority to use, value, possession and entry.

(9) *Domestic Relations Matters.* The court's consideration of a report or recommendation submitted by the friend of the court pursuant to MCL 552.505(1)(g) or (h).

(10)   *Mental Health Hearings.* In hearings under Chapters 4, 4A, 5, and 6 of the Mental Health Code, MCL 330.1400 *et seq.,* the court may consider hearsay data that are part of the basis for the opinion presented by a testifying mental health expert.

Rule 1102 Title

These rules are named the Michigan Rules of Evidence and may be cited as MRE.

The notes following the individual rules were drafted by the chair and the reporter of the committee which drafted the proposed rules of evidence for the benefit of the bench and bar and are not authoritative constructions by the Court.

Made in the USA
Monee, IL
10 July 2021